Gratitude Miracles

the 5-minute journal that could change everything!

Joyce Wycoff
Flying Ears Press

Copyright (c) Joyce Wycoff, 2016, ALL RIGHTS RESERVED. No part of this book may be reproduced or transmitted in any form or by any means, electronic or mechanical, including photocopying, recording, or by an information storage system without permission from the author at jwycoff@me.com.

Gratitude Miracles, the 5-minute journal that could change everything!

First published: August, 2016

ISBN-13:978-1535592581

Other books by Joyce Wycoff:

Fiction:
- *Sarana's Gift*, a novella
- *Yellowstone Howling, Book 1: It Changes Everything* (Series), in progress

Non Fiction:
- *To Do ... Doing ... Done! A Creative Approach to Managing Projects & Effectively Finishing What Matters Most (Simon & Schuster)* with G. Lynne Snead
- *Mindmapping, Your Personal Guide to Exploring Creativity and Problem-Solving (Berkley Books)*
- *Innovation Training (ASTD)*, with Ruth Ann Hattori
- *Transformation Thinking (Berkley Books)*
- *Breakthrough Selling (Prentice-Hall)*, with Barry Farber
- *Joy after the Fire*, memoir (Self-Published)

Blog: http://joycewycoff.com
Blog: http://gratitudemiracles.com

Cover and interior Photos: Joyce Wycoff, unless otherwise noted

for

for all the people I never thanked:
the authors, the teachers, the artists, the carpenters,
the fighters of fires, the doctors of disease,
those who built the roads through the mountains and deserts,
those who grew the vegetables and fruits for my table,
all the meals and makers-of-meals who went unblessed,
all the garments and sewers and sellers of them that kept me dressed,
and the thousands, millions, of other unthanked souls
who have made my life possible.

for all the beauty I forgot to acknowledge:
the sunrises, rainbows, beaches, forests, flowers and frogs,
the mountains, meadows, moonglows and manatees,
the soft summer days, the snow-covered pines,
the cactus blossoms of spring, the yellow aspens of fall,
all the trees I never thanked for my breath,
all the clouds I never thanked for their beckonings,
all the rocks I never thanked for their stories,
all the rivers and lakes, puddles and ponds,
the oceans of water that refreshed my days,
never once asking for my thanks.

for all the people who made me laugh:
the jokesters, punsters, actors, writers, designers of Tilt-a-Whirls,
all you bubbling fountains of mirth that brought forth
giggles and guffaws, chuckles and chortles,
and graciously accepted them as payment enough.

to all of you, friends and family,
those recognized and total strangers,
finally and utterly incompletely,
thanks. ... Thanks! ... Thank YOU!

*"If the only prayer you said was thank you,
that would be enough."*
— Meister Eckhart

*"One thread connects
us all."*
— Maureen Doallas

*"When you are grateful,
fear disappears and abundance appears."*
— Anthony Robbins

The Basics

Life is a do-it-yourself project.
No one can do it for you.
Same for gratitude.

Gratitude creates miracles.
(Not the walk-on-water, win-the-lottery type of miracles ...
the unexpected-delights-that-make-you-happy-to-be-alive type.)
Only *you* can define what's a miracle for you,
but if it makes you say, "Oh, Wow!" with a smile on your face,
it probably is one. Count it!

This is a DIY book only YOU can write.
It will take about 2-5 MINUTES per day.
Are miracles worth it?

Gratitude: being thankful, viewing life as a wonder-filled gift.

Backstory: Why this journal?

I've lived a long, relatively easy life; long enough to be pulled this way and that; long enough to experience loss and success, joy and pain and know that all of them have made me who I am.

From my early days I've tried to figure things out: big things like science and religion, small things like where love goes when it dies and how a caterpillar turns into a butterfly.

Somewhere, early on, I discovered that I like to boil things down to their essence. When I heard that the Bible could be summarized into one word ... love ... I was ecstatic. I could forget the shoulds and shouldn'ts and just focus on living that one word ... which, of course, is not such a simple thing.

One word: Gratitude

As I grew older, life got more complicated and I kept looking for "the way." I tried this practice and that, and several others. One day I realized that, once again, the essentials of all the wisdom and recommendations of the teachers and gurus could be boiled down to one word: *gratitude.*

For years I circled around gratitude, talking about it, writing about it, collecting quotes about it. The one thing I didn't do was practice it. I thought I was, of course. I thought I was completely committed to it. I said "thank you" often, and tried to notice all the blessings of my life.

One morning I woke up knowing it was time to truly practice gratitude, and everywhere I turned, experts said I needed to keep a gratitude journal.

There are numerous recent studies about gratitude and one thing that surprised me was that *how* you journal about gratitude makes a significant difference. This might surprise you, too.

**Writing 3-5 reasons why you're grateful for ONE thing
is better than just
writing a list of what you're grateful for.**

That surprising bit of information sent me into a frenzy of research to see what other processes would make gratitude journaling more effective.

Because I wanted to get started immediately, I put some forms together and started using them, finding out what worked and what didn't. Then I invited a few friends to use them and got more feedback.

This journal is a result of all of their feedback and suggestions.

I am a practical person. I wanted, and continue to want, the benefits of gratitude ... more happiness, better health, stronger relationships, more joy in life.

From the beginning, I wanted a criteria for judging the success of this practice, and quickly decided that it should be *Miracles*. Not the walking-on-water or winning the lottery type of miracles. More of the surprising delights that seem to come on their own through little or no effort of my own.

How delighted I was when, shortly after starting to keep the gratitude journal, they started showing up ... an invitation to stay with a friend at the beach ... meeting some new friends and knowing almost immediately that they were "family" ... finding the perfect stepping stones for my garden when I didn't even know I was looking for them ... even some unexpected money.

And, the more I noticed these delightful miracles, the more they seemed to show up. And, the more they showed up, the more grateful I became ... creating a positive cycle that just needed to be shared.

Thus, this journal!

Gratitude: being thankful, viewing life as a wonder-filled gift.

The Blog: http://www.GratitudeMiracles.com

Researchers are learning more about gratitude every day ... far too much to put into a journal such as this, so we have created a blog where you can find new research and the writings and thoughts of teachers and experts.

Follow the blog by email and you won't miss the periodic updates. And, please feel free to leave your comments and suggestions. I would love to know about your miracles and your experience with the journal.

Some researchers are beginning to say that the benefits of practicing gratitude are unlimited. Amit Amin at happierhuman.com created the graphic below which makes us think they may be right. They say there are no panaceas in life, however, practicing gratitude might be as close as you can come.

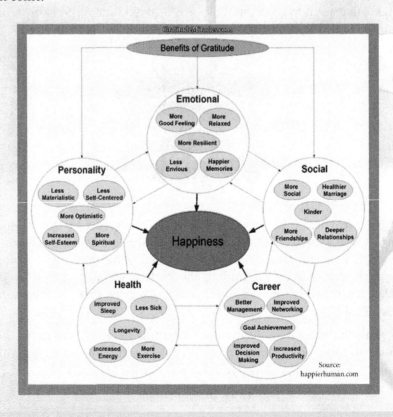

Miracles: unexpected delights that make you say, "Wow!"

Simple as 1-2-3

Your *Gratitude Miracles* journal is set up in thirteen 4-week cycles, one year, to give you enough time to engage the practice of gratitude and fully develop the benefits of that practice.

Each cycle focuses on an important benefit of practicing gratitude and contains the following:

- **2 benefit ponder pages** with questions
- **4-weeks of forms** for recording gratitudes and miracle
- **a cycle summary of gratitudes and miracles** for easy review and to help you see patterns.
- **reflection page** to capture learnings and inspirations

Two days are slightly different:

"Hard" days - some things in our lives are more challenging than others, but it is important to be grateful for them since they are part of what makes us who we are. Call them life lessons or just stuff that we survived and, therefore, made us stronger. Learning to be grateful for them is important.

"You" days - for gratitudes related to you personally: your body, your strengths, your character, your accomplishments and so on.

Miracles: It's helpful to make notes of your miracles as you notice them. Definitions of gratitude and miracles are at the top of each page.

5 Minutes: Think of one thing you're grateful for and spend five minutes each day writing about it on the journal forms.

If you decide to use the gratitudes and miracles summary sheets (highly recommended), you can do them daily, weekly, or anytime you want to remember or review.

1. Pick a gratitude each day and write 3-5 specifics about it.
2. Watch for and record miracles.
3. Repeat

Gratitude: being thankful, viewing life as a wonder-filled gift.

Benefits of Gratitude

Cycle 1 - Happiness

Cycle 2 - Health & Fitness

Cycle 3 - Better Relationships

Cycle 4 - More Success

Cycle 5 - Enhanced Energy

Cycle 6 - Deeper Connection

Cycle 7 - Wonder

Cycle 8 - Peace & Contentment

Cycle 9 - Creativity

Cycle 10 - Stronger Resilience

Cycle 11 - Passion & Purpose

Cycle 12 - Optimism & Generosity

Cycle 13 - Easier Forgiveness

Cycle 1 - Gratitude Creates Happiness

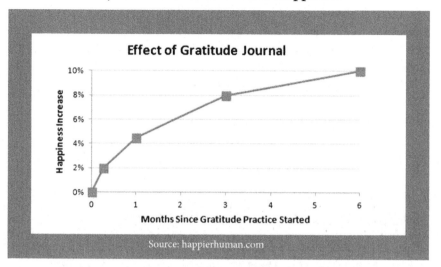

University of California at Davis researcher Robert Emmons states, "The best way to reap the benefits of gratitude is to notice new things you're grateful for every day. Gratitude journaling works because it slowly changes the way we perceive situations by adjusting what we focus on. While you might always be thankful for your great family, just writing 'I'm grateful for my family' week after week doesn't keep your brain on alert for fresh grateful moments.

"Opening your eyes to more of the world around you can deeply enhance your gratitude practice. Make a game out of noticing new things each day.

"Our relationships with others are the greatest determinant of our happiness. So it makes sense to think of other people as we build our gratitude." Emmons suggests that focusing our gratitude on people for whom we're thankful rather than circumstances or material items will enhance the benefits we experience. And while you're at it, why not include others directly into your expression of gratitude? One Happify.com activity involves writing a gratitude letter to someone who had an impact on you whom you've never properly thanked.

Throughout this journal, you will hear from dozens of researchers, writers and philosophers who have thought deeply about gratitude. You can also read more at GratitudeMiracles.com

Gratitude: being thankful, viewing life as a wonder-filled gift.

Cycle 1 - Happiness

Questions to Ponder:
... What does happiness mean to you?
... What makes you happy?
... What does it feel like when you're happy?
... What are you feeling at this moment? If you're not happy right now, what could you do to change that feeling?

Write about your own happiness and feel free to come back to these pages as you go through this cycle.

Happiness is a feeling of joyful anticipation + appreciation. SO MANY Things make me happy - my husband, my children, my friends; my cats, my home, my view; my photography, painting, poetry, + playwriting; good food, good books, good TV shows + movies; colors, dreams, health, games ...

Miracles: **unexpected delights that make you say, "Wow!"**

Cycle 1 - Gratitude Creates Happiness

All the prompts, tasks, suggestions, thoughts and tips in the following pages are there simply to stimulate your thinking.

POET is a useful memory trick to help you remember gratitudes related to People, Opportunities, Experiences and Things.

Use them if they're useful; leave them if they're not.

Gratitude: being thankful, viewing life as a wonder-filled gift.

Happiness Week 1: __3/19/23_____ (Date)

Every day, I will write 3-5 reasons why I'm grateful for ONE thing.
Prompts: apple, angels, air, argument, POET* or your choice.

Day of week: __Sunday__ I'm grateful for __Joanna__
She gets me, appreciates me; we speak the same language + wear the same shoes; she's a constant model of vitality + faith

Day of week: __Monday__ It's hard, but I'm grateful for _____
Bad days painting: they keep me humble + give me textures to paint over later

Day of week: __Tuesday__ I'm grateful for __Christine,__
who explained that to combine swoops + geometric figures represents Chris + me co-existing together so happily

Day of week: __Wednesday__ I'm grateful for my own __creativity__
... and wrote another poem today

Note to self: __Having Pete Amens here to listen to our stories was lovely. Listening is such a gift!...__

Cycle 1 - Happiness

Miracles: **unexpected delights that make you say, "Wow!"**

*"Her whole life shifted
the day she started to tell the truth
about what made her happy."*
-- Brian Andreas

Day of week: Thursday **I'm grateful for** Pete's visit
It was good to be reminded of the stellar bits of Chris's career - and great, now, to have the house to myself ♡

Day of week: Friday **I'm grateful for** Friendship
coffee w/ Patti + lunch w/ Jorie - a good day! Love these women ♡

Day of week: Saturday **I'm grateful for** my kitties, who are so affectionate + amusing, and for all the free books at the library.

Miracles: What miracles and gifts have shown up in my life?
Pete's decision to visit us, his purchase of my photo, + the friendships made thru art.

Tip: Find a gratitude partner. Sharing what you are grateful for is a powerful way to reinforce your own gratitude and stimulate ideas for new gratitudes for each other.

Task: Watch the GratitudeRevealed.com short video on Happiness (1:36). This is a great site to explore for more about gratitude.

Gratitude: being thankful, viewing life as a wonder-filled gift.

Happiness Week 2: __3/26/23_____ (Date)

Every day, I will write 3-5 reasons why I'm grateful for ONE thing.
Prompts: boy, beach, breath, book, POET* or your choice.

Day of week: Sunday   I'm grateful for Frank Gehry
His buildings + the way they use + fill space inspire me; I love the colors + the shapes + the metallic surfaces

Day of week: Monday   It's hard, but I'm grateful for Aging
Not just because it's better than the alternative, but because it keeps us humble + gives us something to chuckle about

Day of week: Tuesday   I'm grateful for those mornings
when I wake up + he wakes up too, and we cuddle a bit. So much love. And then to see the color in the sunrise over the mtn. Bliss!

Day of week: Wednesday   I'm grateful for my own ability to
write, because it still seems to work when everything else gets a little flaky. Plus it seems to bring joy to others...

Note to self: Just because you had a bad couple of days in the studio + almost missed being in a show doesn't mean you're losing it. You just have a lot on your plate.

Miracles: unexpected delights that make you say, "Wow!"

"Let us be grateful to the people who make us happy;
they are the charming gardeners who make our souls blossom."
-- Marcel Proust

Day of week: Thursday **I'm grateful for** The joy I find in painting + in being inspired by other artists, and especially for all the shades of blue :)

Day of week: Friday **I'm grateful for** all the days my foot doesn't hurt; when I can walk + stand + sit with ease + comfort - because today that's not an option.

Day of week: Saturday **I'm grateful for** Fred Oldfield's daughter + her passion for art education for children. A reminder that individuals can make a huge difference in the world.

Miracles: What miracles and gifts have shown up in my life?
Peggy + Kate + Christine being so appreciative of my paintings. Brunch with KC + Dylan :) Anita Feng's buddha. All our wonderful neighbors. The Abstract group. Chris Brady. Mardy Pearl. The Fata Morgana. And my shadow painting which turned out so well for Northwind.

Story: Physician, comedian and social activist Patch Adams says, "At the age of 18, I made up my mind to never have another bad day in my life. I dove into an endless sea of gratitude from which I've never emerged."

Task: Acknowledge someone who helped you who might not be aware of their impact on you.

Gratitude: being thankful, viewing life as a wonder-filled gift.

Happiness Week 3: 4/2/2023 _____ (Date)

Every day, I will write 3-5 reasons why I'm grateful for ONE thing.
Prompts: car, courage, color, conflict, POET* or your choice.

Day of week: Sunday   I'm grateful for the urge to paint + the love of color

Day of week: Monday   It's hard, but I'm grateful for that nothing was seriously damaged by our roof leak + it didn't hit the tax prep materials!

Day of week: Tuesday   I'm grateful for Chris Brady dealing with the roof + all the permit delays. I'm trying to be grateful I didn't get into the Anacortes show. I'm very grateful for Patti, Carol, + Ann + Eve. So blessed.

Day of week: Wednesday   I'm grateful for my own ability to rise above disappointments + find the positive in events + people — and for the luxury of friends to whom I can safely whine!

Note to self: There is so much joy in my life right now — just think of disappointment (Anacortes rejection) as leavening to keep me balanced + appreciative.

Cycle 1 - Happiness

Miracles: unexpected delights that make you say, "Wow!"

"Piglet noticed that even though he had a Very Small Heart, it could hold a rather large amount of Gratitude."
-- A.A. Milne, Winnie-the-Pooh

Day of week: _Thursday_ I'm grateful for _staying calm in the midst of all the craziness - cleaners, asbestos guys, landscapers, Chris, painters, etc._

Day of week: _Friday_ I'm grateful for _a relatively quiet day_

Day of week: _Saturday_ I'm grateful for _Chris's willingness to drive me to Lynden, + Christine's appreciation - and purchases - of my paintings_

Miracles: What miracles and gifts have shown up in my life?
Christine's perceptiveness re my art, + her generosity.
booked a painter for the house
... a guy to lift up the great room

Tip: 10 Minute Clutter Reduction. Clutter causes stress and seems to have a life of its own. Set a timer for 10 minutes and declutter one area. Give thanks for that small, peaceful place.

Task: Try shinrin-yoku, Japanese for forest bathing ... a slow, deliberate immersion in nature.

Gratitude: **being thankful, viewing life as a wonder-filled gift.**

Happiness Week 4: _4/10/23_ (Date)

Every day, I will write 3-5 reasons why I'm grateful for ONE thing.
Prompts: dream, dance, dessert, divorce, POET* or your choice.

Day of week: Monday I'm grateful for the permit approval - now we can move forward + protect that room

Day of week: Tuesday It's hard, but I'm grateful for Northwind for pushing me out of my comfort zone.

Day of week: Wednesday I'm grateful for Vicky and her decision to skip the WPW luncheon, and for Lynn + my fans at the gallery

Day of week: Thursday I'm grateful for my own willingness to be vulnerable to Carol + Ann + Jodie, and my determination to find equitable solutions to the challenges faces the district opens

Note to self: _____

Cycle 1 - Happiness

Miracles: **unexpected delights that make you say, "Wow!"**

*"Happiness is a butterfly, which, when pursued,
is always just beyond your grasp, but which,
if you will sit down quietly, may alight upon you."*
-- Nathaniel Hawthorne

Day of week: Friday   **I'm grateful for** Pamela's decision to trust me with the abstract critique issues

Day of week: Saturday   **I'm grateful for** my beautiful granddaughter, her dad + step mom, and her dad's parents; love them all — such a great visit in spite of the weather

Day of week: Sunday   **I'm grateful for** my goofy friendship with Ken Hulick, + his promise to give precedence to my paintings

Miracles: What miracles and gifts have shown up in my life?
Fans! Purchases! Grandchild! In-laws! The cats are eating again! My painting will be featured at the gallery!

Thought: Albert Camus tells us, "There can be no happiness if the things we believe in are different from the things we do."

Task: Tell someone something specific you like about them.

Gratitude: being thankful, viewing life as a wonder-filled gift.

Happiness Summary:
Brief reminders of gratitudes

	Week 1	Week 2
Day: Sunday	Joanna	Frank gehry Buddy
Day: monday	mistakes + bad paintings	aging humbles us
Day: tues	Christine: Swoops + geometrics	morning cuddles + sunrise
Day: ~~wed~~ Thur	Pete Amons	ability to write
Day: thurs	Patti + Joe	other artists, painting, shades of value
Day: Fri (wed)	Creativity	
Day: Sat	affectionate cats	

Cycle 1 - Happiness

Miracles: unexpected delights that make you say, "Wow!"

Happiness Summary:
Brief reminders of gratitudes

	Week 3	Week 4
Day:	color	Permit approval
Day:	Chris fixing roof	Northwind
Day:	friends	Skyping w/ Wendi
Day:	ability to rise above disappointment	Open Discussion w/ friends
Day:	calm in chaos	Pamela's trust
Day:	quiet day	granddaughter + her grandparents
Day:	more paint purchase	Ken Hulick

Gratitude: being thankful, viewing life as a wonder-filled gift.

Happiness Miracles Summary

Wk #	Brief summary of miracles and transformations

Miracles: unexpected delights that make you say, "Wow!"

Happiness Miracles Summary

Wk #	Brief summary of miracles and transformations

Gratitude: being thankful, viewing life as a wonder-filled gift.

Reflection

What did I learn?
What surprised me?
What would I like to change?

Miracles: unexpected delights that make you say, "Wow!"

Cycle 2 - Gratitude Improves Health & Fitness

Studies have shown that people who regularly practice feeling thankful have a leg up when it comes to their health. Robert Emmons, a psychology professor at the University of California at Davis, has been a leading researcher in this growing field, termed "positive psychology." His research has found that those who adopt an "attitude of gratitude" as a permanent state of mind experience many health benefits.

Deepak Chopra says, "Experiencing gratitude is one of the most effective ways of getting in touch with your soul. When you're in touch with your soul, you eavesdrop on the thoughts of the universe. You feel connected to everything in creation. You embrace the wisdom of uncertainty and you sense yourself as a field of infinite possibilities."

Whether you consider gratitude a practical practice or a spiritual practice, studies show that it affects almost every aspect of your being.

Read more at GratitudeMiracles.com

Gratitude: **being thankful, viewing life as a wonder-filled gift.**

Cycle 2 - Health & Fitness

Questions to Ponder:
... How do you feel about your health and fitness?
... Do you wake up in the morning rested and ready for the day?
... Do you worry about your health?
... Are you at peace with your body?
... Are there things you would like to change about your health and fitness?

Write about your own health and fitness and feel free to come back to these pages as you go through this cycle.

Miracles: **unexpected delights that make you say, "Wow!"**

Cycle 2 - Gratitude Improves Health & Fitness

All the prompts, tasks, suggestions, thoughts and tips in the following pages are there simply to stimulate your thinking.

POET is a useful memory trick to help you remember gratitudes related to People, Opportunities, Experiences and Things.

Use them if they're useful; leave them if they're not.

Gratitude: being thankful, viewing life as a wonder-filled gift.

Health & Fitness Week 1: _____ (Date)

Every day, I will write 3-5 reasons why I'm grateful for ONE thing.
Prompts: energy, earth, engagement, ear, POET* or your choice.

Day of week: _____ I'm grateful for _____
_____
_____
_____
_____

Day of week: _____ It's hard, but I'm grateful for _____
_____
_____
_____
_____

Day of week: _____ I'm grateful for _____
_____
_____
_____
_____

Day of week: _____ I'm grateful for my own _____
_____
_____
_____

Note to self: _____
_____
_____
_____
_____

Cycle 2 - Health & Fitness

Miracles: unexpected delights that make you say, "Wow!"

*"I keep my mind focused on peace,
harmony, health, love and abundance.
Then, I can't be distracted by doubt, anxiety or fear."*
-- Edith Armstrong

Day of week: _____ I'm grateful for _____
_____
_____
_____

Day of week: _____ I'm grateful for _____
_____
_____
_____

Day of week: _____ I'm grateful for _____
_____
_____
_____

Miracles: What miracles and gifts have shown up in my life?
_____
_____
_____

Thought: Wayne Dyer suggests, "Give yourself a gift of five minutes of contemplation in awe of everything you see around you. Go outside and turn your attention to the many miracles there. This five-minute-a-day regimen of appreciation and gratitude will help you to focus your life in awe."

Task: Acknowledge yourself for something you did well.

Gratitude: **being thankful, viewing life as a wonder-filled gift.**

Health & Fitness Week 2: _____ (Date)

Every day, I will write 3-5 reasons why I'm grateful for ONE thing.
Prompts: friends, freedom, faith, fool, POET* or your choice.

Day of week: _____ I'm grateful for _____
_____
_____
_____
_____

Day of week: _____ It's hard, but I'm grateful for _____
_____
_____
_____
_____

Day of week: _____ I'm grateful for _____
_____
_____
_____
_____

Day of week: _____ I'm grateful for my own _____
_____
_____
_____

Note to self: _____
_____
_____
_____

Miracles: **unexpected delights that make you say, "Wow!"**

*"In health there is freedom.
Health is the first of all liberties."*
-- Henri Frederic Amiel

Day of week: _____ I'm grateful for _____

Day of week: _____ I'm grateful for _____

Day of week: _____ I'm grateful for _____

Miracles: What miracles and gifts have shown up in my life?

Thought: Studies show gratitude actually makes people want to exercise more and take care of their health.

Task: How could you make someone smile?

Gratitude: **being thankful, viewing life as a wonder-filled gift.**

Health & Fitness Week 3: _____ (Date)

Every day, I will write 3-5 reasons why I'm grateful for ONE thing.
Prompts: give, garage, garden, game, POET* or your choice.

Day of week: _____ I'm grateful for _____

_____
_____
_____

Day of week: _____ It's hard, but I'm grateful for _____

_____
_____
_____

Day of week: _____ I'm grateful for _____

_____
_____
_____

Day of week: _____ I'm grateful for my own _____

_____
_____
_____

Note to self: _____

_____
_____
_____

Miracles: unexpected delights that make you say, "Wow!"

"When we give cheerfully and accept gratefully, everyone is blessed."
-- Maya Angelou

Day of week: _____ I'm grateful for _____

_____

_____

Day of week: _____ I'm grateful for _____

_____

_____

Day of week: _____ I'm grateful for _____

_____

_____

Miracles: What miracles and gifts have shown up in my life?

_____

_____

_____

_____

_____

Thought: How often do you say "thank you" to yourself? Why don't you say thanks to yourself more often?

Task: What do you like best about your spouse, friend or child?

Gratitude: **being thankful, viewing life as a wonder-filled gift.**

Health & Fitness Week 4: _____ (Date)

Every day, I will write 3-5 reasons why I'm grateful for ONE thing.
Prompts: health, hope, house, habit, POET* or your choice.

Day of week: _____ I'm grateful for _____

_____
_____
_____
_____

Day of week: _____ It's hard, but I'm grateful for _____

_____
_____
_____
_____

Day of week: _____ I'm grateful for _____

_____
_____
_____
_____

Day of week: _____ I'm grateful for my own _____

_____
_____
_____

Note to self: _____

_____
_____
_____

Cycle 2 - Health & Fitness   **36**

Miracles: unexpected delights that make you say, "Wow!"

*"Blessed are the flexible,
for they shall not be bent out of shape."*
-- Anonymous

Day of week: _____ I'm grateful for _____
_____
_____
_____

Day of week: _____ I'm grateful for _____
_____
_____
_____

Day of week: _____ I'm grateful for _____
_____
_____
_____

Miracles: What miracles and gifts have shown up in my life?
_____
_____
_____
_____

Quote: Oprah says, "Be thankful for what you have; you'll end up having more. If you concentrate on what you don't have, you will never, ever have enough."

Task: Come up with 10 answers to the question: "One way life is loving me right now is …."

Gratitude: being thankful, viewing life as a wonder-filled gift.

Health & Fitness Summary:
Brief reminders of gratitudes

	Week 1	Week 2
Day:		
Day:		
Day:		
Day:		
Day:		
Day:		
Day:		

Miracles: unexpected delights that make you say, "Wow!"

Health & Fitness Summary:
Brief reminders of gratitudes

	Week 3	Week 4
Day:		
Day:		
Day:		
Day:		
Day:		
Day:		
Day:		

Gratitude: being thankful, viewing life as a wonder-filled gift.

Health & Fitness Miracles Summary

Wk #	Brief summary of miracles and transformations

Miracles: unexpected delights that make you say, "Wow!"

Health & Fitness Miracles Summary

Wk #	Brief summary of miracles and transformations

Gratitude: being thankful, viewing life as a wonder-filled gift.

Reflection

What did I learn?
What surprised me?
What would I like to change?

Cycle 3 - Gratitude Builds Better Relationships

A new study shows that feelings of gratitude were the most consistent predictor of marital quality among couples of all ages and socioeconomic backgrounds. Couples who are more grateful for one another report being closer, more committed, and having greater mutual relationship satisfaction.

Maria Hillel says that the benefits of greater gratitude within relationships include:

"You can more easily accept others and yourself. We are all imperfect people seeking the best possible life. There is no reason not to be friends.

"You no longer take anything personally. Life presents difficult challenges for everyone; it's not just about you."

For more information, go to GratitudeMiracles.com.

Gratitude: **being thankful, viewing life as a wonder-filled gift.**

Cycle 3 - Better Relationships

Questions to Ponder:
… How do you feel about your relationships?
… How do you build love and appreciation with your loved ones?
… What's the balance of criticism and appreciation in your relationships?
… Are there things you would like to change about your relationships?

Write about your own relationships and feel free to come back to these pages as you go through this cycle.

_____

_____

_____

_____

_____

_____

_____

_____

_____

_____

_____

_____

_____

_____

_____

_____

_____

Miracles: **unexpected delights that make you say, "Wow!"**

Cycle 3 - Gratitude Builds Better Relationships

All the prompts, tasks, suggestions, thoughts and tips in the following pages are there simply to stimulate your thinking.

POET is a useful memory trick to help you remember gratitudes related to People, Opportunities, Experiences and Things.

Use them if they're useful; leave them if they're not.

Gratitude: **being thankful, viewing life as a wonder-filled gift.**

Better Relationships Week 1: _____ (Date)

Every day, I will write 3-5 reasons why I'm grateful for ONE thing.
Prompts: imagination, ink, idol, imperfect, POET* or your choice.

Day of week: _____ I'm grateful for _____
_____
_____
_____

Day of week: _____ It's hard, but I'm grateful for _____
_____
_____
_____

Day of week: _____ I'm grateful for _____
_____
_____
_____

Day of week: _____ I'm grateful for my own _____
_____
_____
_____

Note to self: _____
_____
_____
_____

Cycle 3 - Better Relationships

Miracles: **unexpected delights that make you say, "Wow!"**

"When you arise in the morning, think of what a precious privilege it is to be alive--to breathe, to think, to enjoy, to love ..."
--Marcus Aurelius

Day of week: _____ I'm grateful for _____
_____
_____
_____

Day of week: _____ I'm grateful for _____
_____
_____
_____

Day of week: _____ I'm grateful for _____
_____
_____
_____

Miracles: What miracles and gifts have shown up in my life?
_____
_____
_____
_____

Tip: Gratitude Jars are a way to collect special moments. Simply describe them on a small notes and stash them in a jar. Some people even decorate the jars. Why not?

When times are tough, you have a resource of good moments to help you remember when things were better.

Task: What's the nicest thing someone ever said to you?

Gratitude: being thankful, viewing life as a wonder-filled gift.

Better Relationships Week 2: _____ (Date)

Every day, I will write 3-5 reasons why I'm grateful for ONE thing.
Prompts: joy, justice, jewelry, journal, POET* or your choice.

Day of week: _____ I'm grateful for _____

_____
_____
_____
_____

Day of week: _____ It's hard, but I'm grateful for _____

_____
_____
_____
_____

Day of week: _____ I'm grateful for _____

_____
_____
_____
_____

Day of week: _____ I'm grateful for my own _____

_____
_____

Note to self: _____

_____
_____
_____

Cycle 3 - Better Relationships

Miracles: **unexpected delights that make you say, "Wow!"**

"When we focus on our gratitude, the tide of disappointment goes out and the tide of love rushes in."
-- Kristin Armstrong

Day of week: _____ I'm grateful for _____

_____

_____

_____

Day of week: _____ I'm grateful for _____

_____

_____

_____

Day of week: _____ I'm grateful for _____

_____

_____

_____

Miracles: What miracles and gifts have shown up in my life?

_____

_____

_____

Thought: Karl Barth says, "Joy is the simplest form of gratitude." And, David Steindl Rast says, "The root of joy is gratefulness. It is not joy that makes us grateful; it is gratitude that makes us joyful." Either way, gratitude and joy are intertwined.

Task: Think of a memory from your childhood that brings you joy and feelings of gratitude. You might want to write a bit more about on one of your journal days.

Gratitude: **being thankful, viewing life as a wonder-filled gift.**

Better Relationships Week 3: _____ (Date)

Every day, I will write 3-5 reasons why I'm grateful for ONE thing.
Prompts: kindness, kale, knot, key, POET* or your choice.

Day of week: _____ I'm grateful for _____

Day of week: _____ It's hard, but I'm grateful for _____

Day of week: _____ I'm grateful for _____

Day of week: _____ I'm grateful for my own _____

Note to self: _____

Cycle 3 - Better Relationships

Miracles: unexpected delights that make you say, "Wow!"

"I don't have to chase extraordinary moments to find happiness - it's right in front of me if I'm paying attention and practicing gratitude."
-- Brene Brown

Day of week :_____ I'm grateful for _____

_____

_____

Day of week: _____ I'm grateful for _____

_____

_____

Day of week: _____ I'm grateful for _____

_____

_____

Miracles: What miracles and gifts have shown up in my life?

_____

_____

_____

_____

Thought: Melodie Beattie tells us, "Gratitude unlocks the fullness of life. It turns what we have into enough, and more. It turns denial into acceptance, chaos into order, confusion to clarity. It can turn a meal into a feast, a house into a home, a stranger into a friend."

Task: Find a way to compliment a stranger.

Gratitude: **being thankful, viewing life as a wonder-filled gift.**

Better Relationships Week 4: _____ (Date)

Every day, I will write 3-5 reasons why I'm grateful for ONE thing.
Prompts: love, light, laughter, lie, POET* or your choice.

Day of week: _____ I'm grateful for _____
_____
_____
_____
_____

Day of week: _____ It's hard, but I'm grateful for _____
_____
_____
_____
_____

Day of week: _____ I'm grateful for _____
_____
_____
_____
_____

Day of week: _____ I'm grateful for my own _____
_____
_____
_____

Note to self: _____
_____
_____
_____

Miracles: unexpected delights that make you say, "Wow!"

> *"The deepest craving of human nature is the need to be appreciated."*
> -- William James

Day of week: _____ I'm grateful for _____

_____

_____

Day of week: _____ I'm grateful for _____

_____

_____

Day of week: _____ I'm grateful for _____

_____

_____

Miracles: What miracles and gifts have shown up in my life?

_____

_____

_____

Suggestion: Ralph Waldo Emerson suggested that we "Cultivate the habit of being grateful for every good thing that comes to you, and to give thanks continuously. And because all things have contributed to your advancement, you should include all things in your gratitude."

Task: Take time to savor a favorite food. Really taste it and think about all the people who grew it, packaged it, delivered it to you for your enjoyment.

Gratitude: being thankful, viewing life as a wonder-filled gift.

Better Relationships Summary:
Brief reminders of gratitudes

	Week 1	Week 2
Day:		
Day:		
Day:		
Day:		
Day:		
Day:		
Day:		

Miracles: unexpected delights that make you say, "Wow!"

Better Relationships Summary:
Brief reminders of gratitudes

	Week 3	Week 4
Day:		
Day:		
Day:		
Day:		
Day:		
Day:		
Day:		

Gratitude: being thankful, viewing life as a wonder-filled gift.

Better Relationships Miracles Summary

Wk #	Brief summary of miracles and transformations

Miracles: unexpected delights that make you say, "Wow!"

Better Relationships Miracles Summary

Wk #	Brief summary of miracles and transformations

Gratitude: **being thankful, viewing life as a wonder-filled gift.**

Reflection

**What did I learn?
What surprised me?
What would I like to change?**

Miracles: **unexpected delights that make you say, "Wow!"**

Cycle 4 - Gratitude Supports Success

aaronendré

scarcity thinking	abundance thinking
"There will never be enough"	"There will always be more"
Competes to stay on top	Collaborates to stay on top
Hoardes things from others	Generous with others
Won't share knowledge	Shares knowledge
Won't offer help to others	Freely offers help to others
Suspicious of others	Trusts and builds rapport
Resents competition	Welcomes competition
Afraid of being replaced	Strives to grow
Believes times are tough	Believes the best is yet to come
Believes the pie is shrinking	Believes the pie is growing
Thinks small and avoids risk	Thinks big and embraces risk
Fears change	Takes ownership of change

Scarcity thinking vs. Abundance thinking

Gratitude leads to abundance thinking which leads to success.

Dr. Joseph Mercola states, "Science tells us that people who are thankful for what they have are happier and reach their goals with greater ease.

"Your future health and happiness depends largely on the thoughts you think *today*. So each moment of every day is an opportunity to turn your thinking around, thereby helping or hindering your ability to think and feel more positively in the very next moment. Starting and/or ending each day by thinking of something you're grateful for is one way to keep your mind on the right track."

Read more about gratitude and success at GratitudeMiracles.com

Gratitude: **being thankful, viewing life as a wonder-filled gift.**

Cycle 4 - More Success

Questions to Ponder:
... Are you as successful as you would like to be?
... How might being more grateful affect your level of success?
... How could you be a more abundant thinker?

Write about your own successes and general level of success and feel free to come back to these pages as you go through this cycle.

Miracles: **unexpected delights that make you say, "Wow!"**

Cycle 4 - Gratitude Supports Success

All the prompts, tasks, suggestions, thoughts and tips in the following pages are there simply to stimulate your thinking.

POET is a useful memory trick to help you remember gratitudes related to People, Opportunities, Experiences and Things.

Use them if they're useful; leave them if they're not.

Gratitude: **being thankful, viewing life as a wonder-filled gift.**

More Success Week 1: _____ (Date)

Every day, I will write 3-5 reasons why I'm grateful for ONE thing.
Prompts: mind, music, mystery, mandala, POET* or your choice.

Day of week: _____ I'm grateful for _____
_____
_____
_____
_____

Day of week: _____ It's hard, but I'm grateful for _____
_____
_____
_____
_____

Day of week: _____ I'm grateful for _____
_____
_____
_____
_____

Day of week: _____ I'm grateful for my own _____
_____
_____
_____

Note to self: _____
_____
_____
_____

Miracles: **unexpected delights that make you say, "Wow!"**

"Acknowledging the good that you already have in your life is the foundation for all abundance."
— Eckhart Tolle

Day of week: _____ I'm grateful for _____
_____
_____
_____

Day of week: _____ I'm grateful for _____
_____
_____
_____

Day of week: _____ I'm grateful for _____
_____
_____
_____

Miracles: What miracles and gifts have shown up in my life?
_____
_____
_____
_____

Tip: Emails are nice, phone calls are fleeting but an actual letter can be treasured forever. Write a letter to someone who has meant something special to you.

Task: Give thanks for something that is abundantly "free."

Gratitude: **being thankful, viewing life as a wonder-filled gift.**

More Success Week 2: _____ (Date)

Every day, I will write 3-5 reasons why I'm grateful for ONE thing.
Prompts: nature, now, napkin, name, POET* or your choice.

Day of week: _____ I'm grateful for _____

_____

_____

_____

Day of week: _____ It's hard, but I'm grateful for _____

_____

_____

_____

Day of week: _____ I'm grateful for _____

_____

_____

_____

Day of week: _____ I'm grateful for my own _____

_____

_____

Note to self: _____

_____

_____

_____

Miracles: **unexpected delights that make you say, "Wow!"**

"No matter what the situation is ... close your eyes and think of all the things in your life you could be grateful for right now."
-- Deepak Chopra

Day of week: _____ I'm grateful for _____

_____

_____

_____

Day of week: _____ I'm grateful for _____

_____

_____

_____

Day of week: _____ I'm grateful for _____

_____

_____

_____

Miracles: What miracles and gifts have shown up in my life?

_____

_____

_____

_____

Make a List: What six tangible things are most important in your every day life? Specifically, why are you grateful for them?

Task: Take a gratitude stroll around your house, office, backyard or neighborhood. Name two things you're grateful for with each step.

Gratitude: **being thankful, viewing life as a wonder-filled gift.**

More Success Week 3: _____ (Date)

Every day, I will write 3-5 reasons why I'm grateful for ONE thing.
Prompts: open, one, om, oath, POET* or your choice.

Day of week: _____ I'm grateful for _____

_____
_____
_____

Day of week: _____ It's hard, but I'm grateful for _____

_____
_____
_____

Day of week: _____ I'm grateful for _____

_____
_____
_____

Day of week: _____ I'm grateful for my own _____

_____
_____
_____

Note to self: _____

_____
_____
_____

Cycle 4 - Success

Miracles: **unexpected delights that make you say, "Wow!"**

*"The present moment is filled with joy and happiness.
If you are attentive, you will see it."*
— Thich Nhat Hanh

Day of week :_____ I'm grateful for _____

_____

_____

_____

Day of week: _____ I'm grateful for _____

_____

_____

_____

Day of week: _____ I'm grateful for _____

_____

_____

_____

Miracles: What miracles and gifts have shown up in my life?

_____

_____

_____

_____

Thought: Dr. Joseph Mercola says, "Keeping a gratitude journal is a practice recommended by many psychologists, and it can have far-reaching consequences. In one study, people who kept a gratitude journal reported exercising more and logged fewer doctor's visits compared to those who focused on sources of aggravation."

Task: Thank someone who has to work on a holiday.

Gratitude: **being thankful, viewing life as a wonder-filled gift.**

More Success Week 4: _____ (Date)

Every day, I will write 3-5 reasons why I'm grateful for ONE thing.
Prompts: peace, poetry, pray, pale, POET* or your choice.

Day of week: _____ I'm grateful for _____

_____

_____

_____

Day of week: _____ It's hard, but I'm grateful for _____

_____

_____

_____

Day of week: _____ I'm grateful for _____

_____

_____

_____

Day of week: _____ I'm grateful for my own _____

_____

_____

Note to self: _____

_____

_____

_____

Miracles: **unexpected delights that make you say, "Wow!"**

*"Not what we have, but what we enjoy,
constitutes our abundance."*
-- John Petit-Senn

Day of week: _____ I'm grateful for _____
_____
_____
_____

Day of week: _____ I'm grateful for _____
_____
_____
_____

Day of week: _____ I'm grateful for _____
_____
_____
_____

Miracles: What miracles and gifts have shown up in my life?
_____
_____
_____
_____

Thought: Thank your body. When was the last time you thanked your body for taking you through the day, for letting you see, hear, taste, smell and touch the people, beauty and things in your life?

Task: Thank yourself for three accomplishments or kindnesses you've done in the past few days.

Gratitude: being thankful, viewing life as a wonder-filled gift.

More Success Summary:
Brief reminders of gratitudes

	Week 1	Week 2
Day:		
Day:		
Day:		
Day:		
Day:		
Day:		
Day:		

Miracles: unexpected delights that make you say, "Wow!"

More Success Summary:
Brief reminders of gratitudes

	Week 3	Week 4
Day:		
Day:		
Day:		
Day:		
Day:		
Day:		
Day:		

Gratitude: being thankful, viewing life as a wonder-filled gift.

More Success Miracles Summary

Wk #	Brief summary of miracles and transformations

Miracles: unexpected delights that make you say, "Wow!"

More Success Miracles Summary

Wk #	Brief summary of miracles and transformations

Gratitude: being thankful, viewing life as a wonder-filled gift.

Reflection

What did I learn?
What surprised me?
What would I like to change?

_____
_____
_____
_____
_____
_____
_____
_____
_____
_____
_____
_____
_____
_____
_____
_____
_____
_____
_____
_____

Miracles: **unexpected delights that make you say, "Wow!"**

Cycle 5 - Gratitude Boosts Energy

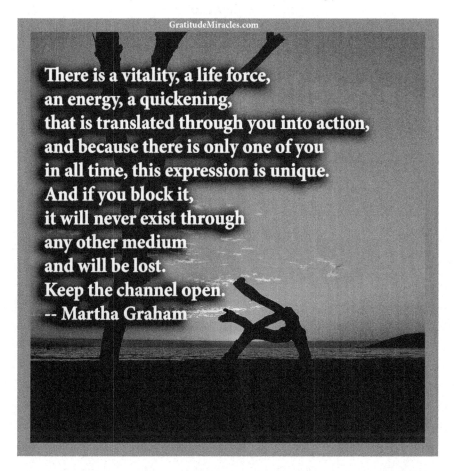

Gratitude shifts our focus to the present moment. Adela Rubio, a "deep dive mentor," states, "Even though the actions, or experiences you might feel grateful for occurred in the past, the energy of gratitude, focuses in the present moment. The present moment is where everything IS! It connects you to what's true, to the dynamic aliveness of right now... the best place to BE!"

Abraham Maslow stated that, "The ability to be in the present moment is a major component of mental wellness."

Gratitude helps us stay in the present and, therefore, be healthier mentally and have more energy for the things we want to do in life.

Read more about gratitude and energy at GratitudeMiracles.com

Gratitude: **being thankful, viewing life as a wonder-filled gift.**

Cycle 5 - Enhanced Energy

Questions to Ponder:
... Do you normally have as much energy as you need to enjoy life?
... What energizes you? What depletes your energy?
... Do you know how to consciously change your energy level?

Write about your own level of energy and feel free to come back to these pages as you go through this cycle.

_____
_____
_____
_____
_____
_____
_____
_____
_____
_____
_____
_____
_____
_____
_____
_____
_____
_____

Miracles: **unexpected delights that make you say, "Wow!"**

Cycle 5 - Gratitude Boosts Energy

All the prompts, tasks, suggestions, thoughts and tips in the following pages are there simply to stimulate your thinking.

POET is a useful memory trick to help you remember gratitudes related to People, Opportunities, Experiences and Things.

Use them if they're useful; leave them if they're not.

Gratitude: **being thankful, viewing life as a wonder-filled gift.**

Enhanced Energy Week 1: _____ (Date)

Every day, I will write 3-5 reasons why I'm grateful for ONE thing.
Prompts: quiet, quest, question, quarter, POET* or your choice.

Day of week: _____ I'm grateful for _____

_____

_____

_____

Day of week: _____ It's hard, but I'm grateful for _____

_____

_____

_____

Day of week: _____ I'm grateful for _____

_____

_____

_____

Day of week: _____ I'm grateful for my own _____

_____

_____

_____

Note to self: _____

_____

_____

_____

Cycle 5 - Enhanced Energy

Miracles: unexpected delights that make you say, "Wow!"

"Energy is a bit like money: if you have a positive balance, you can distribute it in various ways."
-- Stephen Hawking

Day of week: _____ I'm grateful for _____

_____

_____

_____

Day of week: _____ I'm grateful for _____

_____

_____

_____

Day of week: _____ I'm grateful for _____

_____

_____

_____

Miracles: What miracles and gifts have shown up in my life?

_____

_____

_____

_____

Try This: Gratitude Vision: Jafree Ozwald at EnlightenedBeings.com suggests putting on your "Gratitude Glasses" when you wake up in order to see everything in your life with that perspective. Try it. It could completely change your energy.

Task: Thank your eyes for allowing you to see beauty.

Gratitude: **being thankful, viewing life as a wonder-filled gift.**

Enhanced Energy Week 2: _____ (Date)

Every day, I will write 3-5 reasons why I'm grateful for ONE thing.
Prompts: relationship, respect, river, rose, POET* or your choice.

Day of week: _____ I'm grateful for _____
_____
_____
_____

Day of week: _____ It's hard, but I'm grateful for _____
_____
_____
_____

Day of week: _____ I'm grateful for _____
_____
_____
_____

Day of week: _____ I'm grateful for my own _____
_____
_____
_____

Note to self: _____
_____
_____
_____

Miracles: unexpected delights that make you say, "Wow!"

*"The only thing that keeps a person going is energy.
And what is energy but liking life?"*
-- Louis Auchincloss

Day of week: _____ I'm grateful for _____
_____
_____
_____

Day of week: _____ I'm grateful for _____
_____
_____
_____

Day of week: _____ I'm grateful for _____
_____
_____
_____

Miracles: What miracles and gifts have shown up in my life?
_____
_____
_____
_____

Thought: Bruce Campbell reminds us that research shows that we can change our mood by changing the tone of the things we say to ourselves. When our self-talk is negative, it creates negative energy. Focusing on gratitude makes it almost impossible to continue with negative self-talk.

Task: Think of five things that energize you. They should be great candidates for your daily gratitudes.

Gratitude: **being thankful, viewing life as a wonder-filled gift.**

Enhanced Energy Week 3: _____ (Date)

Every day, I will write 3-5 reasons why I'm grateful for ONE thing.
Prompts: story, shadow, safe, survive, POET* or your choice.

Day of week: _____ I'm grateful for _____

_____
_____
_____
_____

Day of week: _____ It's hard, but I'm grateful for _____

_____
_____
_____
_____

Day of week: _____ I'm grateful for _____

_____
_____
_____
_____

Day of week: _____ I'm grateful for my own _____

_____
_____
_____

Note to self: _____

_____
_____
_____

Miracles: **unexpected delights that make you say, "Wow!"**

"Gratitude turns negative energy into positive energy. There is no situation or circumstance so small or large that it is not susceptible to gratitude's power."
-- Melody Beattie

Day of week :_____ I'm grateful for _____

_____

_____

_____

Day of week: _____ I'm grateful for _____

_____

_____

_____

Day of week: _____ I'm grateful for _____

_____

_____

_____

Miracles: What miracles and gifts have shown up in my life?

_____

_____

_____

_____

Thought: Bertran Piccard, the first solo, around the world balloonist, says, "The most renewable energy we have is our potential and our own passion."

Task: Watch the GratitudeRevealed.com short video on Energy (1:36). This is a great site to explore for more about gratitude.

Gratitude: **being thankful, viewing life as a wonder-filled gift.**

Enhanced Energy Week 4: _____ (Date)

Every day, I will write 3-5 reasons why I'm grateful for ONE thing.
Prompts: travel, teach, tree, trust, POET* or your choice.

Day of week: _____ I'm grateful for _____

_____
_____
_____
_____

Day of week: _____ It's hard, but I'm grateful for _____

_____
_____
_____
_____

Day of week: _____ I'm grateful for _____

_____
_____
_____
_____

Day of week: _____ I'm grateful for my own _____

_____
_____
_____

Note to self: _____
_____
_____
_____

Miracles: **unexpected delights that make you say, "Wow!"**

"I crossed the street to walk in the sunshine."
-- Elizabeth Gilbert

Day of week: _____ I'm grateful for _____
_____
_____
_____

Day of week: _____ I'm grateful for _____
_____
_____
_____

Day of week: _____ I'm grateful for _____
_____
_____
_____

Miracles: What miracles and gifts have shown up in my life?
_____
_____
_____
_____

Thought: Robert Emmons, a pioneer in gratitude research, says two obstacles to being grateful are forgetfulness and lack of awareness. You can counter them by giving yourself visual cues that trigger thoughts of gratitude. It could be something you carry or wear, such as a piece of jewelry.

Suggestion: Emmons says he puts Post-It notes listing his blessings in many places, including on his refrigerator, mirrors and the steering wheel of his car.

Gratitude: being thankful, viewing life as a wonder-filled gift.

Enhanced Energy Summary:
Brief reminders of gratitudes

	Week 1	Week 2
Day:		
Day:		
Day:		
Day:		
Day:		
Day:		
Day:		

Miracles: unexpected delights that make you say, "Wow!"

Enhanced Energy Summary:
Brief reminders of gratitudes

	Week 3	Week 4
Day:		
Day:		
Day:		
Day:		
Day:		
Day:		
Day:		

Gratitude: being thankful, viewing life as a wonder-filled gift.

Enhanced Energy Miracles Summary

Wk #	Brief summary of miracles and transformations

Miracles: unexpected delights that make you say, "Wow!"

Enhanced Energy Miracles Summary

Wk #	Brief summary of miracles and transformations

Gratitude: being thankful, viewing life as a wonder-filled gift.

Reflection

What did I learn?
What surprised me?
What would I like to change?

Cycle 6 - Gratitude Builds Connection

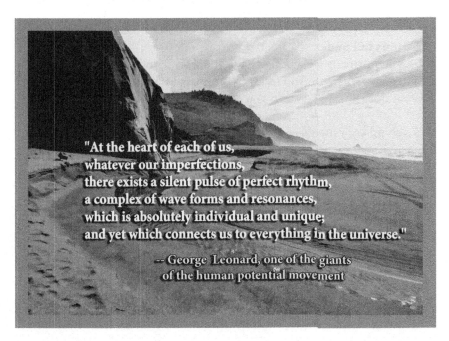

"At the heart of each of us, whatever our imperfections, there exists a silent pulse of perfect rhythm, a complex of wave forms and resonances, which is absolutely individual and unique; and yet which connects us to everything in the universe."

-- George Leonard, one of the giants of the human potential movement

We are part of an interconnected world ... connection to ourselves, to each other, to the world of plants and animals, to the inanimate world of oceans and mountains, rocks and clouds. When we feel gratitude for all of those elements, we build our sense of connection and our sense of peace and belonging in the world.

Yale's Center for Emotional Intelligence says this about practicing gratitude: "Gratitude isn't just an emotion that happens along, but a virtue we can cultivate. Think of it as something you practice as you might meditation or yoga.

"Gratitude practice begins by **paying attention**. Notice all the good things you normally take for granted. Did you sleep well last night? Did someone at work or on the street treat you with courtesy? Have you caught a glimpse of the sky, with its sun and clouds, and had a moment of peace?

"It also involves acknowledging that difficult and painful moments are instructive and you can be grateful for them as well. Directing our attention this way blocks feelings of victimhood."

Read more about gratitude and connection at GratitudeMiracles.com.

Gratitude: **being thankful, viewing life as a wonder-filled gift.**

Cycle 6 - Deeper Connection

Questions to Ponder:
... Do you normally feel connected to the world around you?
... When and where do you feel most connected?
... What does it feel like when you are most connected?

Write about your own feelings of connection and feel free to come back to these pages as you go through this cycle.

Miracles: **unexpected delights that make you say, "Wow!"**

Cycle 6 - Gratitude Builds Connection

All the prompts, tasks, suggestions, thoughts and tips in the following pages are there simply to stimulate your thinking.

POET is a useful memory trick to help you remember gratitudes related to People, Opportunities, Experiences and Things.

Use them if they're useful; leave them if they're not.

Gratitude: **being thankful, viewing life as a wonder-filled gift.**

Deeper Connection Week 1: _____ (Date)

Every day, I will write 3-5 reasons why I'm grateful for ONE thing.
Prompts: union, umbrella, urban, urge, POET* or your choice.

Day of week: _____ I'm grateful for _____

_____

_____

_____

Day of week: _____ It's hard, but I'm grateful for _____

_____

_____

_____

Day of week: _____ I'm grateful for _____

_____

_____

_____

Day of week: _____ I'm grateful for my own _____

_____

_____

_____

Note to self: _____

_____

_____

_____

Cycle 6 - Deeper Connection

Miracles: unexpected delights that make you say, "Wow!"

*"We are all connected. To each other biologically.
To the earth chemically. To the rest of the universe atomically."*
-- Neil deGrasse Tyson

Day of week: _____ I'm grateful for _____
_____
_____
_____

Day of week: _____ I'm grateful for _____
_____
_____
_____

Day of week: _____ I'm grateful for _____
_____
_____
_____

Miracles: What miracles and gifts have shown up in my life?
_____
_____
_____
_____

Thought: Fred Rogers (Mr. Rogers) reports, "When I was a boy and I would see scary things in the news, my mother would say to me, 'Look for the helpers. You will always find people who are helping.'"

Task: Listen to a bird sing and say, "Thank you!"

Gratitude: **being thankful, viewing life as a wonder-filled gift.**

Deeper Connection Week 2: _____ (Date)

Every day, I will write 3-5 reasons why I'm grateful for ONE thing.
Prompts: vacation, voice, value, vision, POET* or your choice.

Day of week: _____ I'm grateful for _____

_____
_____
_____

Day of week: _____ It's hard, but I'm grateful for _____

_____
_____
_____

Day of week: _____ I'm grateful for _____

_____
_____
_____

Day of week: _____ I'm grateful for my own _____

_____
_____

Note to self: _____

_____
_____
_____

Cycle 6 - Deeper Connection

Miracles: **unexpected delights that make you say, "Wow!"**

"There isn't a person alive on Earth who couldn't use a connection with nature."
-- Nalini Nadkarni

Day of week: _____ I'm grateful for _____

_____

_____

Day of week: _____ I'm grateful for _____

_____

_____

Day of week: _____ I'm grateful for _____

_____

_____

Miracles: What miracles and gifts have shown up in my life?

_____

_____

_____

Thought: Mark Zuckerberg, founder of Facebook says, "Facebook was not originally created to be a company. It was built to accomplish a social mission--to make the world more open and connected."

Task: Start all gatherings ... meals, meetings, coffee klatches ... with a ritual of sharing gratitudes before meals.

Gratitude: **being thankful, viewing life as a wonder-filled gift.**

Deeper Connection Week 3: _____ (Date)

Every day, I will write 3-5 reasons why I'm grateful for ONE thing.
Prompts: water, walk, words, wonder, POET* or your choice.

Day of week: _____ I'm grateful for _____

_____

_____

_____

_____

Day of week: _____ It's hard, but I'm grateful for _____

_____

_____

_____

_____

Day of week: _____ I'm grateful for _____

_____

_____

_____

_____

Day of week: _____ I'm grateful for my own _____

_____

_____

_____

Note to self: _____

_____

_____

_____

Cycle 6 - Deeper Connection

Miracles: **unexpected delights that make you say, "Wow!"**

*"Joy is what happens to us
when we allow ourselves
to recognize how good things really are."*
-- Marianne Williamson

Day of week :_____ I'm grateful for _____

_____

_____

Day of week: _____ I'm grateful for _____

_____

_____

Day of week: _____ I'm grateful for _____

_____

_____

Miracles: What miracles and gifts have shown up in my life?

_____

_____

Suggestion: Rabbi Nahman suggests this: "Find a day for yourself—better yet, late at night. Go to the forest or to the field, or lock yourself in a room ... You will meet solitude there. There you will be able to listen attentively to the noise of the wind first, to birds singing, to see wonderful nature and to notice yourself in it ... and to come back to harmonic connection with the world and its Creator."

Task: Appreciate the first beautiful thing you see in the morning.

Gratitude: **being thankful, viewing life as a wonder-filled gift.**

Deeper Connection Week 4: _____ (Date)

Every day, I will write 3-5 reasons why I'm grateful for ONE thing.
Prompts: listen, intuition, circle, clean, POET* or your choice.

Day of week: _____ I'm grateful for _____

_____

_____

_____

Day of week: _____ It's hard, but I'm grateful for _____

_____

_____

_____

Day of week: _____ I'm grateful for _____

_____

_____

_____

Day of week: _____ I'm grateful for my own _____

_____

_____

_____

Note to self: _____

_____

_____

_____

Miracles: unexpected delights that make you say, "Wow!"

*"Zen pretty much comes down to three things:
everything changes, everything is connected, pay attention."*
-- Jane Hirshfield

Day of week: _____ I'm grateful for _____
_____
_____
_____

Day of week: _____ I'm grateful for _____
_____
_____
_____

Day of week: _____ I'm grateful for _____
_____
_____
_____

Miracles: What miracles and gifts have shown up in my life?
_____
_____
_____
_____

Thought: Albert Einstein said it is an optical delusion of our mind that we think we are separate. "This separateness is like a prison for us. Our job is to widen the circle of our compassion so we feel connected with all people and situations."

Task: Thank your skin for holding all your cells in place and protecting you from the dirt and grime, heat and cold of the world.

Gratitude: being thankful, viewing life as a wonder-filled gift.

Deeper Connection Summary:
Brief reminders of gratitudes

	Week 1	Week 2
Day:		
Day:		
Day:		
Day:		
Day:		
Day:		
Day:		

Miracles: unexpected delights that make you say, "Wow!"

Deeper Connection Summary:
Brief reminders of gratitudes

	Week 3	Week 4
Day:		
Day:		
Day:		
Day:		
Day:		
Day:		
Day:		

Gratitude: being thankful, viewing life as a wonder-filled gift.

Deeper Connection Miracles Summary

Wk #	Brief summary of miracles and transformations

Miracles: unexpected delights that make you say, "Wow!"

Deeper Connection Miracles Summary

Wk #	Brief summary of miracles and transformations

Gratitude: being thankful, viewing life as a wonder-filled gift.

Reflection

What did I learn?
What surprised me?
What would I like to change?

Miracles: unexpected delights that make you say, "Wow!"

Cycle 7 - Gratitude Creates Wonder

"We are all born with a sense of wonder.
Wonder and awe allow us to transcend the ordinary.
Wonder inspires us to open our hearts and our minds
to engender gratitude."
-- Louis Schwartzberg

One of the most popular gratitude quotes comes from G. K. Chesterton (shown on Week 2). One of his that is not as well known, but is equally great is: "You say grace before meals. All right.

"But I say grace before the concert and the opera, and grace before the play and pantomime, and grace before I open a book, and grace before sketching, painting, swimming, fencing, boxing, walking, playing, dancing and grace before I dip the pen in the ink."

The American Chesterton Society says he was the greatest writer of the 20th century because he was also the greatest thinker of the 20th century. Obviously he steeped himself in gratitude.

More about gratitude and wonder at GratitudeMiracles.com.

Gratitude: **being thankful, viewing life as a wonder-filled gift.**

Cycle 7 - Wonder

Questions to Ponder:

... What makes you feel awe and wonder?
... What is filled with wonder in your every day life?
... What wonders would you like to have more of in your life?

Write about your own feelings of wonder and feel free to come back to these pages as you go through this cycle.

Miracles: **unexpected delights that make you say, "Wow!"**

Cycle 7 - Gratitude Creates Wonder

All the prompts, tasks, suggestions, thoughts and tips in the following pages are there simply to stimulate your thinking.

POET is a useful memory trick to help you remember gratitudes related to People, Opportunities, Experiences and Things.

Use them if they're useful; leave them if they're not.

Gratitude: **being thankful, viewing life as a wonder-filled gift.**

Wonder Week 1: _____ (Date)

Every day, I will write 3-5 reasons why I'm grateful for ONE thing.
Prompts: yoga, youth, yellow, yam, POET* or your choice.

Day of week: _____ I'm grateful for _____
_____
_____
_____

Day of week: _____ It's hard, but I'm grateful for _____
_____
_____
_____

Day of week: _____ I'm grateful for _____
_____
_____
_____

Day of week: _____ I'm grateful for my own _____
_____
_____
_____

Note to self: _____
_____
_____

Miracles: **unexpected delights that make you say, "Wow!"**

"I would maintain that thanks are the highest form of thought, and that gratitude is happiness doubled by wonder."
-- G.K. Chesterton

Day of week: _____ I'm grateful for _____

_____

_____

_____

Day of week: _____ I'm grateful for _____

_____

_____

_____

Day of week: _____ I'm grateful for _____

_____

_____

_____

Miracles: What miracles and gifts have shown up in my life?

_____

_____

_____

Why do we travel?
*"People travel to wonder at the height of mountains, at the huge waves of the sea, at the long courses of rivers, at the vast compass of the ocean, at the circular motion of the stars; and they pass by themselves
... without wondering."*
-- St. Augustine

Gratitude: **being thankful, viewing life as a wonder-filled gift.**

Wonder Week 2: _____ (Date)

Every day, I will write 3-5 reasons why I'm grateful for ONE thing.
Prompts: zen, zone, zucchini, zest, POET* or your choice.

Day of week:_____ I'm grateful for _____

_____

_____

_____

Day of week: _____ It's hard, but I'm grateful for _____

_____

_____

_____

Day of week:_____ I'm grateful for _____

_____

_____

_____

Day of week: _____ I'm grateful for my own _____

_____

_____

_____

Note to self: _____

_____

_____

_____

Miracles: unexpected delights that make you say, "Wow!"

"The meaning I picked, the one that changed my life:
Overcome fear, behold wonder."
-- Richard Bach

Day of week: _____ I'm grateful for _____

_____

_____

Day of week: _____ I'm grateful for _____

_____

_____

Day of week: _____ I'm grateful for _____

_____

_____

Miracles: What miracles and gifts have shown up in my life?

_____

_____

_____

Thought: e.e. cummings said, "We do not believe in ourselves until someone reveals that something deep inside us is valuable, worth listening to, worthy of our trust, sacred to our touch.

"Once we believe in ourselves, we can risk curiosity, wonder, spontaneous delight or any experience that reveals the human spirit."

Task: Express wonder that trees breathe out what we breathe in.

Gratitude: **being thankful, viewing life as a wonder-filled gift.**

Wonder Week 3: _____ (Date)

Every day, I will write 3-5 reasons why I'm grateful for ONE thing.
Prompts: art, ancestor, abundance, awe, POET* or your choice.

Day of week: _____ I'm grateful for _____

_____

_____

_____

Day of week: _____ It's hard, but I'm grateful for _____

_____

_____

_____

Day of week: _____ I'm grateful for _____

_____

_____

_____

Day of week: _____ I'm grateful for my own _____

_____

_____

Note to self: _____

_____

_____

_____

Miracles: unexpected delights that make you say, "Wow!"

"What can we say beyond Wow, in the presence of glorious art, in music so magnificent that it can't have originated solely on this side of things? Wonder takes our breath away, and makes room for new breath."
-- Anne Lamott

Day of week :_____ I'm grateful for _____

_____

_____

_____

Day of week:_____ I'm grateful for _____

_____

_____

_____

Day of week:_____ I'm grateful for _____

_____

_____

_____

Miracles: What miracles and gifts have shown up in my life?

_____

_____

_____

_____

Suggestion: Deepak Chopra tells us Rabbi Baruch Spinoza, in the seventeenth century, suggested that each day for a month, we ask ourselves the following three questions:

- *Who or what inspired me today?*
- *What brought me happiness today?*
- *What brought me comfort and deep peace today?*

Gratitude: **being thankful, viewing life as a wonder-filled gift.**

Wonder Week 4: _____ (Date)

Every day, I will write 3-5 reasons why I'm grateful for ONE thing.
Prompts: blue, beauty, bird, broken, POET* or your choice.

Day of week: _____ I'm grateful for _____

_____

_____

_____

Day of week: _____ It's hard, but I'm grateful for _____

_____

_____

_____

Day of week: _____ I'm grateful for _____

_____

_____

_____

Day of week: _____ I'm grateful for my own _____

_____

_____

Note to self: _____

_____

_____

_____

Miracles: **unexpected delights that make you say, "Wow!"**

"Wisdom begins in wonder."
-- Socrates

Day of week: _____ I'm grateful for _____

_____

_____

_____

Day of week: _____ I'm grateful for _____

_____

_____

_____

Day of week: _____ I'm grateful for _____

_____

_____

_____

Miracles: What miracles and gifts have shown up in my life?

_____

_____

_____

_____

Thought: In current terminology, gratitude is a "life hack" and Maria Hill at lifehack.org says: "Gratitude is not a feeling. It is really a way of life and a way of meeting life and all of its challenges.

"Gratitude is a frame for reality, which enables us to align with the good in the world as well as the evolutionary progress of the human race. It is the opposite of resentful entitlement. Gratitude allows us to accept things as they are even as we try to improve them. It enables us to see ourselves as participants in creating the good in life."

Gratitude: being thankful, viewing life as a wonder-filled gift.

Wonder Summary:
Brief reminders of gratitudes

	Week 1	Week 2
Day:		
Day:		
Day:		
Day:		
Day:		
Day:		
Day:		

Miracles: unexpected delights that make you say, "Wow!"

Wonder Summary:

Brief reminders of gratitudes

	Week 3	Week 4
Day:		
Day:		
Day:		
Day:		
Day:		
Day:		
Day:		

Gratitude: being thankful, viewing life as a wonder-filled gift.

Wonder Miracles Summary

Wk #	Brief summary of miracles and transformations

Miracles: unexpected delights that make you say, "Wow!"

Wonder Miracles Summary

Wk #	Brief summary of miracles and transformations

Gratitude: **being thankful, viewing life as a wonder-filled gift.**

Reflection

**What did I learn?
What surprised me?
What would I like to change?**

Cycle 8 - Gratitude Sows Peace & Contentment

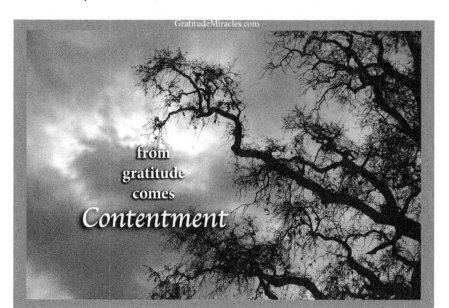

It is easy to be grateful for what we have.

The harder question is how to be content with what we don't have. To say, "This is enough." Being grateful for every aspect of our lives creates a pathway to contentment.

Joshua Becker at BecomingMinimalist.com says, "Gratitude provides proper understanding of our place in the world. Gratitude is the feeling and expression of thankfulness for the actions of others that are costly to them and beneficial to us.

"By definition, gratitude requires humility. It requires us to admit we have been the recipient of something we did not deserve. And it calls us to admit there are no entirely self-made men or women.

"**Gratitude opens the door to contentment.** It pushes our praise to those who rightly deserve it. It causes us to focus on the good things we already have regardless of our present circumstances. It improves our well-being in almost every regard. As a result, it is the surest pathway to contentment."

More about gratitude and Peace & Contentment at GratitudeMiracles.com.

Gratitude: **being thankful, viewing life as a wonder-filled gift.**

Cycle 8 - Peace & Contentment

Questions to Ponder:
... How content with your life are you?
... What "lacks" disturb your contentment? And, how might you find contentment and peace with those situations?
... How and when do you feel most content?

Write about your own feelings of Peace & Contentment and feel free to come back to these pages as you go through this cycle.

Miracles: **unexpected delights that make you say, "Wow!"**

Cycle 8 - Gratitude Sows Peace & Contentment

All the prompts, tasks, suggestions, thoughts and tips in the following pages are there simply to stimulate your thinking.

POET is a useful memory trick to help you remember gratitudes related to People, Opportunities, Experiences and Things.

Use them if they're useful; leave them if they're not.

Gratitude: being thankful, viewing life as a wonder-filled gift.

Peace & Contentment Week 1: _____ (Date)

Every day, I will write 3-5 reasons why I'm grateful for ONE thing.
Prompts: children, cat, clock, change, POET* or your choice.

Day of week: _____ I'm grateful for _____
_____
_____
_____

Day of week: _____ It's hard, but I'm grateful for _____
_____
_____
_____

Day of week: _____ I'm grateful for _____
_____
_____
_____

Day of week: _____ I'm grateful for my own _____
_____
_____

Note to self: _____
_____
_____
_____

Miracles: **unexpected delights that make you say, "Wow!"**

*"The miracle is not to walk on water.
The miracle is to walk on the green earth in the present moment,
to appreciate the peace and beauty that are available now."
-- Thich Nhat Hanh*

Day of week: _____ I'm grateful for _____
_____
_____
_____

Day of week: _____ I'm grateful for _____
_____
_____
_____

Day of week: _____ I'm grateful for _____
_____
_____
_____

Miracles: What miracles and gifts have shown up in my life?
_____
_____
_____

Contentment Defined: at peace with our place in the world, with the family and friends who surround us, the material possessions we have accumulated, and the life situation we are living. It is a satisfaction with what we have, a sense of having enough and being enough.

Task: Thank the glass of water you're drinking for saving your life.

Gratitude: **being thankful, viewing life as a wonder-filled gift.**

Peace & Contentment Week 2: _____ (Date)

Every day, I will write 3-5 reasons why I'm grateful for ONE thing.
Prompts: desire, destroy, depth, death, POET* or your choice.

Day of week: _____ I'm grateful for _____

_____

_____

_____

Day of week: _____ It's hard, but I'm grateful for _____

_____

_____

_____

Day of week: _____ I'm grateful for _____

_____

_____

_____

Day of week: _____ I'm grateful for my own _____

_____

_____

_____

Note to self: _____

_____

_____

_____

Miracles: **unexpected delights that make you say, "Wow!"**

"A musician must make music, an artist must paint, a poet must write,
if he is to be ultimately at peace with himself.
What one can be, one must be."
-- Abraham Maslow

Day of week: _____ I'm grateful for _____
_____
_____
_____

Day of week: _____ I'm grateful for _____
_____
_____
_____

Day of week: _____ I'm grateful for _____
_____
_____
_____

Miracles: What miracles and gifts have shown up in my life?
_____
_____
_____
_____

Suggestion: Mick Ukleja at LeadershipTraq.com suggests that you "***Saunter into your day.*** The word saunter comes from the Middle Ages. Everything was considered sainted, including the earth – St. Terre. Therefore, to saunter is *to walk on the earth with reverence for its holiness.*" Take time to enter your day slowly and with reverence.

Task: Thank your brain.

Gratitude: **being thankful, viewing life as a wonder-filled gift.**

Peace & Contentment Week 3: _____ (Date)

Every day, I will write 3-5 reasons why I'm grateful for ONE thing.
Prompts: enter, east, evil, early, POET* or your choice.

Day of week: _____ I'm grateful for _____

_____
_____
_____

Day of week: _____ It's hard, but I'm grateful for _____

_____
_____
_____

Day of week: _____ I'm grateful for _____

_____
_____
_____

Day of week: _____ I'm grateful for my own _____

_____
_____
_____

Note to self: _____

_____
_____
_____

Cycle 8 - Wonder

Miracles: **unexpected delights that make you say, "Wow!"**

"Until you make peace with who you are,
you'll never be content with what you have."
-- Doris Mortman

Day of week :_____ I'm grateful for _____

_____

_____

Day of week: _____ I'm grateful for _____

_____

_____

Day of week: _____ I'm grateful for _____

_____

_____

Miracles: What miracles and gifts have shown up in my life?

_____

_____

_____

Suggestion: John Muir urges us to "Climb the mountains and get their good tidings; nature's peace will flow into you as sunshine into flowers; the winds will blow their freshness into you and the storms their energy; and cares will drop off like autumn leaves." And, for all those things you can feel great gratitude.

Tip: Give gratitude for the unseen bacteria that keeps us healthy.

Gratitude: **being thankful, viewing life as a wonder-filled gift.**

Peace & Contentment Week 4: _____ (Date)

Every day, I will write 3-5 reasons why I'm grateful for ONE thing.
Prompts: family, flowers, fire, false, POET* or your choice.

Day of week: _____ I'm grateful for _____
_____
_____
_____

Day of week: _____ It's hard, but I'm grateful for _____
_____
_____
_____

Day of week: _____ I'm grateful for _____
_____
_____
_____

Day of week: _____ I'm grateful for my own _____
_____
_____
_____

Note to self: _____
_____
_____
_____

Cycle 8 - Wonder

Miracles: **unexpected delights that make you say, "Wow!"**

*"He who is not contented with what he has,
would not be contented with what he would like to have."*
-- Socrates

Day of week: _____ I'm grateful for _____
_____
_____
_____

Day of week: _____ I'm grateful for _____
_____
_____
_____

Day of week: _____ I'm grateful for _____
_____
_____
_____

Miracles: What miracles and gifts have shown up in my life?
_____
_____
_____
_____

Thought: My dog, Missy, is content. She doesn't care anything about having a bigger, more beautiful house with a view. She doesn't even seem to need a better roommate.

She does want more treats, of course, and her daily walks, and she has no problem asking for them, but she takes it in stride, and still loves me when they are slow in coming. As far as I can tell, she's completely at peace with herself and her world. What a teacher! *Who's your teacher?*

Gratitude: being thankful, viewing life as a wonder-filled gift.

Peace & Contentment Summary:
Brief reminders of gratitudes

	Week 1	Week 2
Day:		
Day:		
Day:		
Day:		
Day:		
Day:		
Day:		

Miracles: unexpected delights that make you say, "Wow!"

Peace & Contentment Summary:
Brief reminders of gratitudes

	Week 3	Week 4
Day:		
Day:		
Day:		
Day:		
Day:		
Day:		
Day:		

Gratitude: being thankful, viewing life as a wonder-filled gift.

Peace & Contentment Miracles Summary

Wk #	Brief summary of miracles and transformations

Miracles: unexpected delights that make you say, "Wow!"

Peace & Contentment Miracles Summary

Wk #	Brief summary of miracles and transformations

Gratitude: being thankful, viewing life as a wonder-filled gift.

Reflection

What did I learn?
What surprised me?
What would I like to change?

Miracles: **unexpected delights that make you say, "Wow!"**

Cycle 9 - Gratitude Stimulates Creativity

"Gratitude opens the door to the power, the wisdom, the creativity of the universe."
-- Deepak Chopra

Expressing gratitude for everything in our lives opens us up, makes us look at things in a different way, noticing details, understanding the interrelationships. It keeps us in the moment. We can't worry about an unpaid bill when we're thinking about all the ways we're grateful for the new rose in our garden.

That kind of attention is fundamental to problem-solving and creativity. The positive regard that we feel when we're practicing gratitude makes us see things in new ways. A well-worn story in creativity tells us about a man walking through a field of burrs. Rather than rant and rail about the discomfort and inconvenience of being stuck, he thought, "Wow! Look how those little hooks catch my socks." And, thus, velcro was born.

The more we practice gratitude, the more we will notice details and connections that will lead to ideas. And, while all ideas are gifts, not all of them are good ones. Honor them when they come, but be prepared to sort the keepers from the losers.

More about gratitude and Creativity at GratitudeMiracles.com.

Gratitude: **being thankful, viewing life as a wonder-filled gift.**

Cycle 9 - Creativity

Questions to Ponder:
... The question is not: Are you creative? It's HOW are you creative?
... What are you normally doing when ideas come to you?
... Do you write your ideas down when they come to you?
(Supposedly Confucius said: *short pencil better than long memory.*)

Write about your own process of Creativity and feel free to come back to these pages as you go through this cycle.

Miracles: **unexpected delights that make you say, "Wow!"**

Cycle 9 - Gratitude Stimulates Creativity

All the prompts, tasks, suggestions, thoughts and tips in the following pages are there simply to stimulate your thinking.

POET is a useful memory trick to help you remember gratitudes related to People, Opportunities, Experiences and Things.

Use them if they're useful; leave them if they're not.

Gratitude: **being thankful, viewing life as a wonder-filled gift.**

Creativity Week 1: _____ (Date)

Every day, I will write 3-5 reasons why I'm grateful for ONE thing.
Prompts: grace, gems, groan, green, POET* or your choice.

Day of week: _____ I'm grateful for _____

_____

_____

_____

Day of week: _____ It's hard, but I'm grateful for _____

_____

_____

_____

Day of week: _____ I'm grateful for _____

_____

_____

_____

Day of week: _____ I'm grateful for my own _____

_____

_____

_____

Note to self: _____

_____

_____

_____

Cycle 9 - Creativity

Miracles: **unexpected delights that make you say, "Wow!"**

*"I am in awe of the human spirit.
We are such amazing beings. Filled with light.
With possibility. Hope. Creativity. Joy. Love."
-- M. L. Gallagher*

Day of week: _____ I'm grateful for _____

_____
_____
_____

Day of week: _____ I'm grateful for _____

_____
_____
_____

Day of week: _____ I'm grateful for _____

_____
_____
_____

Miracles: What miracles and gifts have shown up in my life?
_____
_____
_____

Creativity Defined: Humans are creative beings. We all have the ability to transcend traditional ideas, rules, patterns, relationships, or the like, and to create meaningful new ideas, forms, methods, interpretations. We all have imagination and the ability to put originality into our lives, our work, our relationships, our world.

Task: Thank a teacher from your present or past.

Gratitude: **being thankful, viewing life as a wonder-filled gift.**

Creativity Week 2: _____ (Date)

Every day, I will write 3-5 reasons why I'm grateful for ONE thing.
Prompts: hand, healing, horse, help, POET* or your choice.

Day of week: _____ I'm grateful for _____

_____

_____

_____

Day of week: _____ It's hard, but I'm grateful for _____

_____

_____

_____

Day of week: _____ I'm grateful for _____

_____

_____

_____

Day of week: _____ I'm grateful for my own _____

_____

_____

Note to self: _____

_____

_____

_____

Miracles: **unexpected delights that make you say, "Wow!"**

*"Originality lives at the crossroads,
at the point where world and self open to each other
in the transparence in the night rain."*
-- Jane Hirshfield

Day of week: _____ I'm grateful for _____

_____
_____
_____

Day of week: _____ I'm grateful for _____

_____
_____
_____

Day of week: _____ I'm grateful for _____

_____
_____
_____

Miracles: What miracles and gifts have shown up in my life?

_____
_____
_____

Thought: Maja at BusinessInRhyme.com says, "Gratitude can help us combat fear and anxiety. That feeling of appreciation opens the door for receiving even better things to flow into your life – like creativity. Experience of positive emotions and nurturing the state of well-being helps us engage in the activities that encourage discovery and growth. Your observation improves; your relationship with the environment improves and you tackle problems from different angles."

Task: Imagine walking through a rainbow and tasting the colors.

Gratitude: **being thankful, viewing life as a wonder-filled gift.**

Creativity Week 3: _____ (Date)

Every day, I will write 3-5 reasons why I'm grateful for ONE thing.
Prompts: idea, iris, intention, image, POET* or your choice.

Day of week: _____ I'm grateful for _____
_____
_____
_____

Day of week: _____ It's hard, but I'm grateful for _____
_____
_____
_____

Day of week: _____ I'm grateful for _____
_____
_____
_____

Day of week: _____ I'm grateful for my own _____
_____
_____
_____

Note to self: _____
_____
_____
_____

Miracles: **unexpected delights that make you say, "Wow!"**

*"If people never did silly things,
nothing intelligent would ever be done."*
-- Ludwig Wittgenstein

Day of week: _____ I'm grateful for _____

_____

_____

Day of week: _____ I'm grateful for _____

_____

_____

Day of week: _____ I'm grateful for _____

_____

_____

Miracles: What miracles and gifts have shown up in my life?

_____

_____

_____

Thought: Gratitude raises our spirit into the realm of play and joy. Carl Jung once said, "The creation of something new is not accomplished by the intellect but by the play instinct acting from inner necessity. The creative mind plays with objects it loves." Gratitude reminds us of what we love.

Remember: What was your favorite toy as a child?

Gratitude: **being thankful, viewing life as a wonder-filled gift.**

Creativity Week 4: _____ (Date)

Every day, I will write 3-5 reasons why I'm grateful for ONE thing.
Prompts: juice, jade, jump, jail, POET* or your choice.

Day of week: _____ I'm grateful for _____

_____

_____

_____

Day of week: _____ It's hard, but I'm grateful for _____

_____

_____

_____

Day of week: _____ I'm grateful for _____

_____

_____

_____

Day of week: _____ I'm grateful for my own _____

_____

_____

_____

Note to self: _____

_____

_____

_____

Miracles: **unexpected delights that make you say, "Wow!"**

*"Sometimes I think creativity is magic;
it's not a matter of finding an idea, but allowing the idea to find you."*
-- Maya Lin

Day of week: _____ I'm grateful for _____

_____

_____

_____

Day of week: _____ I'm grateful for _____

_____

_____

_____

Day of week: _____ I'm grateful for _____

_____

_____

_____

Miracles: What miracles and gifts have shown up in my life?

_____

_____

_____

_____

Thought: Teresa Amabile at the Harvard School of Business states, "The desire to do something because you find it deeply satisfying and personally challenging inspires the highest levels of creativity, whether it's in the arts, sciences, or business." Keeping a gratitude journal helps you identify those things you love and find inspiring.

Task: Find joy in smell ... a baby's head, a new puppy, rosemary, mint, a freshly-opened rose.

Gratitude: being thankful, viewing life as a wonder-filled gift.

Creativity Summary:
Brief reminders of gratitudes

	Week 1	Week 2
Day:		
Day:		
Day:		
Day:		
Day:		
Day:		
Day:		

Miracles: unexpected delights that make you say, "Wow!"

Creativity Summary:

Brief reminders of gratitudes

	Week 3	Week 4
Day:		
Day:		
Day:		
Day:		
Day:		
Day:		
Day:		

Gratitude: being thankful, viewing life as a wonder-filled gift.

Creativity Miracles Summary

Wk #	Brief summary of miracles and transformations

Miracles: unexpected delights that make you say, "Wow!"

Creativity Miracles Summary

Wk #	Brief summary of miracles and transformations

Gratitude: being thankful, viewing life as a wonder-filled gift.

Reflection

**What did I learn?
What surprised me?
What would I like to change?**

Cycle 10 - Gratitude Strengthens Resilience

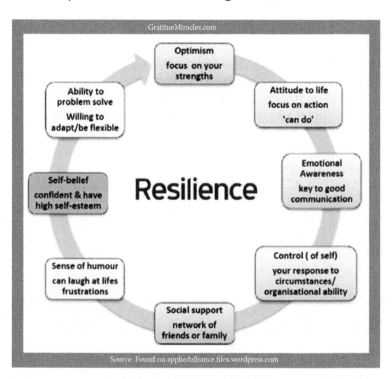

Canadian life coach Ray Samuels defines resilience as "functioning with a sense of purpose, meaning and forward momentum in the face of trauma."

An example of that kind of trauma was featured in the commencement speech to UC Berkeley graduates in 2016. Sheryl Sandberg, Chief Operating Officer at Facebook, told her story of the unexpected death of her husband, her family's grief, and what she learned in the aftermath.

"Dave's death changed me in very profound ways. I learned about the depths of sadness and the brutality of loss. But I also learned that when life sucks you under, you can kick against the bottom, break the surface, and breathe again. I learned that in the face of the void—or in the face of any challenge—you can choose joy and meaning."

Links to read or watch Sheryl Sandberg's often humorous and tech-savvy speech are available at GratitudeMiracles.com along with more about gratitude and resilience.

Gratitude: being thankful, viewing life as a wonder-filled gift.

Cycle 10 - Stronger Resilience

Questions to Ponder:
... How resilient are you? Do you "bounce back" after difficulties.
... Do you know how to calm yourself during chaotic times?
... How do you react to unexpected difficulties?
   * If you would like to test your resiliency, go to ResiliencyQuiz.com

Write about your own feelings of resilience and feel free to come back to these pages as you go through this cycle.

Miracles: **unexpected delights that make you say, "Wow!"**

Cycle 10 - Gratitude Strengthens Resilience

All the prompts, tasks, suggestions, thoughts and tips in the following pages are there simply to stimulate your thinking.

POET is a useful memory trick to help you remember gratitudes related to People, Opportunities, Experiences and Things.

Use them if they're useful; leave them if they're not.

Gratitude: **being thankful, viewing life as a wonder-filled gift.**

Stronger Resilience Week 1: _____ (Date)

Every day, I will write 3-5 reasons why I'm grateful for ONE thing.
Prompts: keen, kiss, kill, kitchen, POET* or your choice.

Day of week: _____ I'm grateful for _____
_____
_____
_____
_____

Day of week: _____ It's hard, but I'm grateful for _____
_____
_____
_____
_____

Day of week: _____ I'm grateful for _____
_____
_____
_____
_____

Day of week: _____ I'm grateful for my own _____
_____
_____
_____

Note to self: _____
_____
_____
_____

Miracles: **unexpected delights that make you say, "Wow!"**

"It's the hard days — the days that challenge you to your very core — that will determine who you are."
-- Sheryl Sandberg

Day of week: _____ I'm grateful for _____

_____

_____

_____

Day of week: _____ I'm grateful for _____

_____

_____

_____

Day of week: _____ I'm grateful for _____

_____

_____

_____

Miracles: What miracles and gifts have shown up in my life?

_____

_____

_____

Thought: Martin Seligman, Founder and Director of the Positive Psychology Center, University of Pennsylvania, says, "Life inflicts the same setbacks and tragedies on the optimist as on the pessimist, but the optimist weathers them better." Gratitude supports optimism.

Task: Thank your community for something free that brings you pleasure.

Gratitude: **being thankful, viewing life as a wonder-filled gift.**

Stronger Resilience Week 2: _____ (Date)

Every day, I will write 3-5 reasons why I'm grateful for ONE thing.
Prompts: loss, loan, letter, labyrinth, POET* or your choice.

Day of week:_____ I'm grateful for _____

_____
_____
_____

Day of week: _____ It's hard, but I'm grateful for _____

_____
_____
_____

Day of week:_____ I'm grateful for _____

_____
_____
_____

Day of week: _____ I'm grateful for my own _____

_____
_____
_____

Note to self: _____

_____
_____
_____

Miracles: unexpected delights that make you say, "Wow!"

"I don't measure a man's success by how high he climbs, but how high he bounces when he hits bottom."
-- George S. Patton, Jr.

Day of week: _____ I'm grateful for _____

_____

_____

Day of week: _____ I'm grateful for _____

_____

_____

Day of week: _____ I'm grateful for _____

_____

_____

Miracles: What miracles and gifts have shown up in my life?

_____

_____

Thought: Robert Emmons, the world's leading scientific expert on gratitude says that, in troubling times, "not only will a grateful attitude help—it is *essential*. In fact, it is precisely under crisis conditions when we have the most to gain by a grateful perspective on life. In the face of demoralization, gratitude has the power to energize. In the face of brokenness, gratitude has the power to heal. In the face of despair, gratitude has the power to bring hope. In other words, gratitude can help us cope with hard times."

Task: Say thanks for the feel of the warm sun on your skin.

Gratitude: **being thankful, viewing life as a wonder-filled gift.**

Stronger Resilience Week 3: _____ (Date)

Every day, I will write 3-5 reasons why I'm grateful for ONE thing.
Prompts: meditation, mouse, mountain, move, POET* or your choice.

Day of week: _____ I'm grateful for _____

___

___

___

___

Day of week: _____ It's hard, but I'm grateful for _____

___

___

___

___

Day of week: _____ I'm grateful for _____

___

___

___

___

Day of week: _____ I'm grateful for my own _____

___

___

___

Note to self: _____

___

___

___

Miracles: **unexpected delights that make you say, "Wow!"**

*"It is not the strongest of the species that survive,
nor the most intelligent,
but the one most responsive to change."*
-- Charles Darwin

Day of week :_____ I'm grateful for _____

_____

_____

Day of week: _____ I'm grateful for _____

_____

_____

Day of week: _____ I'm grateful for _____

_____

_____

Miracles: What miracles and gifts have shown up in my life?

_____

_____

_____

_____

Story: Nick Vujicic says, "Often people ask how I manage to be happy despite having no arms and no legs. The quick answer is that I have a choice. I can be angry about not having limbs, or I can be thankful that I have a purpose. I chose gratitude."

Task: Give yourself a special treat just because you're you.

Gratitude: **being thankful, viewing life as a wonder-filled gift.**

Stronger Resilience Week 4: _____ (Date)

Every day, I will write 3-5 reasons why I'm grateful for ONE thing.
Prompts: nose, nurture, nasty, never, POET* or your choice.

Day of week: _____ I'm grateful for _____
_____
_____
_____

Day of week: _____ It's hard, but I'm grateful for _____
_____
_____
_____

Day of week: _____ I'm grateful for _____
_____
_____
_____

Day of week: _____ I'm grateful for my own _____
_____
_____

Note to self: _____
_____
_____
_____

Miracles: **unexpected delights that make you say, "Wow!"**

*"Life doesn't get easier or more forgiving;
we get stronger and more resilient."*
-- Steve Maraboli

Day of week: _____ I'm grateful for _____

_____

_____

Day of week: _____ I'm grateful for _____

_____

_____

Day of week: _____ I'm grateful for _____

_____

_____

Miracles: What miracles and gifts have shown up in my life?

_____

_____

Thought: Robert Emmons says, "It is vital to make a distinction between *feeling grateful* and *being grateful*. We don't have total control over our emotions. We cannot easily will ourselves to feel grateful, less depressed, or happy.

"But being grateful is a choice, a prevailing attitude that endures and is relatively immune to the gains and losses that flow in and out of our lives. This perspective is hard to achieve—but my research says it is worth the effort."

Task: Find something perfect about this moment.

Gratitude: being thankful, viewing life as a wonder-filled gift.

Stronger Resilience Summary:
Brief reminders of gratitudes

	Week 1	Week 2
Day:		
Day:		
Day:		
Day:		
Day:		
Day:		
Day:		

Cycle 10 - Stronger Resilience

Miracles: unexpected delights that make you say, "Wow!"

Stronger Resilience Summary:
Brief reminders of gratitudes

	Week 3	Week 4
Day:		
Day:		
Day:		
Day:		
Day:		
Day:		
Day:		

Gratitude: being thankful, viewing life as a wonder-filled gift.

Stronger Resilience Miracles Summary

Wk #	Brief summary of miracles and transformations

Miracles: unexpected delights that make you say, "Wow!"

Stronger Resilience Miracles Summary

Wk #	Brief summary of miracles and transformations

Gratitude: being thankful, viewing life as a wonder-filled gift.

Reflection

What did I learn?
What surprised me?
What would I like to change?

Cycle 11 - Gratitude Clarifies Passion & Purpose

*"When we brim, when we shimmer,
when we glow with love for something, anything,
we become conduits of magic,
and we ourselves become gifts to the world."
-- Melissa Studdard, poet.*

Researchers focused on developing gratitude and purpose among adolescents report, "Whereas gratitude involves recognizing all the good things that someone receives from the world, purpose entails considering how one can contribute to the world around them.

"Indeed, we find these constructs work in tandem; when people feel grateful, they naturally tend to turn towards thinking about how they can give back. In addition, expressing gratitude strengthens relationships, which can then help to guide and support the development of purpose.

"Therefore, we believe that cultivating a deeper sense of gratitude will help individuals to find a sense of purpose in life."

Find more information about gratitude and life purpose at GratitudeMiracles.com

Gratitude: **being thankful, viewing life as a wonder-filled gift.**

Cycle 11 - Passion & Purpose

Questions to Ponder:
... What did you dream of being as a child?
... What do you find yourself doing when you can spare a few minutes?
... Do you believe that your "purpose" has to be your "job?"

Write about your own feelings about Passion and Purpose and feel free to come back to these pages as you go through this cycle.

Miracles: **unexpected delights that make you say, "Wow!"**

Cycle 11 - Gratitude Clarifies Passion & Purpose

All the prompts, tasks, suggestions, thoughts and tips in the following pages are there simply to stimulate your thinking.

POET is a useful memory trick to help you remember gratitudes related to People, Opportunities, Experiences and Things.

Use them if they're useful; leave them if they're not.

Gratitude: **being thankful, viewing life as a wonder-filled gift.**

Passion & Purpose Week 1: _____ (Date)

Every day, I will write 3-5 reasons why I'm grateful for ONE thing.
Prompts: ocean, organ, offer, odor, POET* or your choice.

Day of week: _____ I'm grateful for _____

_____

_____

_____

Day of week: _____ It's hard, but I'm grateful for _____

_____

_____

_____

Day of week: _____ I'm grateful for _____

_____

_____

_____

Day of week: _____ I'm grateful for my own _____

_____

_____

Note to self: _____

_____

_____

_____

Miracles: unexpected delights that make you say, "Wow!"

"Don't ask what the world needs.
Ask what makes you come alive and then go do it.
What the world needs is more people who have come alive."
-- Howard Thurman

Day of week: _____ I'm grateful for _____
_____
_____
_____

Day of week: _____ I'm grateful for _____
_____
_____
_____

Day of week: _____ I'm grateful for _____
_____
_____
_____

Miracles: What miracles and gifts have shown up in my life?
_____
_____
_____

Thought: Poet Melissa Studdard tells an extraordinary love story about a forestry worker/activist in India who began planting trees on a sandbar near a river. For several decades he planted and tended those trees until, gradually, it became a reserve filled with Bengal tigers, Indian rhinoceroses, deer, rabbits, apes, and all kinds of birds. It now covers 1,400 acres. A life purpose ... but did he discover it or create it?

Task: Write yourself a love note.

Gratitude: **being thankful, viewing life as a wonder-filled gift.**

Passion & Purpose Week 2: _____ (Date)

Every day, I will write 3-5 reasons why I'm grateful for ONE thing.
Prompts: pilgrimage, purpose, pink, play, POET* or your choice.

Day of week: _____ I'm grateful for _____

_____
_____
_____

Day of week: _____ It's hard, but I'm grateful for _____

_____
_____
_____

Day of week: _____ I'm grateful for _____

_____
_____
_____

Day of week: _____ I'm grateful for my own _____

_____
_____
_____

Note to self: _____

_____
_____
_____

Miracles: unexpected delights that make you say, "Wow!"

"The purpose that you wish to find in life, like a cure you seek, is not going to fall from the sky. I believe purpose is something for which one is responsible; it's not just divinely assigned."
-- Michael J. Fox

Day of week: _____ I'm grateful for _____

_____

_____

_____

Day of week: _____ I'm grateful for _____

_____

_____

_____

Day of week: _____ I'm grateful for _____

_____

_____

_____

Miracles: What miracles and gifts have shown up in my life?

_____

_____

_____

Thought: Grace Bluerock tells us, "When you live your life in gratitude, you maintain an awareness of all things that are good in your life and focus less on what's not working. When you acknowledge what is going right in your life, it's impossible to become stuck in negativity. Gratitude keeps you thankful, happier, and more positive."

Task: Sit and admire a spot of beauty in your home.

Gratitude: **being thankful, viewing life as a wonder-filled gift.**

Passion & Purpose Week 3: _____ (Date)

Every day, I will write 3-5 reasons why I'm grateful for ONE thing.
Prompts: quick, quote, queen, quiz, POET* or your choice.

Day of week: _____ I'm grateful for _____
_____
_____
_____
_____

Day of week: _____ It's hard, but I'm grateful for _____
_____
_____
_____
_____

Day of week: _____ I'm grateful for _____
_____
_____
_____
_____

Day of week: _____ I'm grateful for my own _____
_____
_____

Note to self: _____
_____
_____
_____

Cycle 11 - Passion & Purpose

Miracles: **unexpected delights that make you say, "Wow!"**

*"Purpose is the place where your
deep gladness meets the world's needs."*
-- Frederick Buechner

Day of week :_____ I'm grateful for _____

_____

_____

_____

Day of week: _____ I'm grateful for _____

_____

_____

_____

Day of week: _____ I'm grateful for _____

_____

_____

_____

Miracles: What miracles and gifts have shown up in my life?

_____

_____

_____

_____

Thought: Wendell Berry says, "It may be that when we no longer know what to do, we have come to our real work, and when we no longer know which way to go, we have begun our real journey. The mind that is not baffled is not employed. The impeded stream is the one that sings."

Question: Margaret Wheatley asks, "Do you think your life's purpose is something you create or discover?"

Gratitude: **being thankful, viewing life as a wonder-filled gift.**

Passion & Purpose Week 4: _____ (Date)

Every day, I will write 3-5 reasons why I'm grateful for ONE thing.
Prompts: retreat, reality, remember, ruin, POET* or your choice.

Day of week: _____ I'm grateful for _____

_____
_____
_____
_____

Day of week: _____ It's hard, but I'm grateful for _____

_____
_____
_____
_____

Day of week: _____ I'm grateful for _____

_____
_____
_____
_____

Day of week: _____ I'm grateful for my own _____

_____
_____
_____

Note to self: _____

_____
_____
_____

Miracles: **unexpected delights that make you say, "Wow!"**

"To love one thing and love it madly is to love everything by default, because mad love is love poured without restraint, and love poured without restraint will always spill over."
-- Melissa Studdard

Day of week: _____ I'm grateful for _____

_____
_____
_____

Day of week: _____ I'm grateful for _____

_____
_____
_____

Day of week: _____ I'm grateful for _____

_____
_____
_____

Miracles: What miracles and gifts have shown up in my life?
_____
_____
_____
_____
_____

Thought: Joseph Campbell said, "If you can see your path laid out in front of you step by step, you know it's not your path. Your own path you make with every step you take. That's why it's your path."

Task: Take time to smell the roses ... and thank them for sharing.

Gratitude: being thankful, viewing life as a wonder-filled gift.

Passion & Purpose Summary:
Brief reminders of gratitudes

	Week 1	Week 2
Day:		
Day:		
Day:		
Day:		
Day:		
Day:		
Day:		

Miracles: unexpected delights that make you say, "Wow!"

Passion & Purpose Summary:
Brief reminders of gratitudes

	Week 3	Week 4
Day:		
Day:		
Day:		
Day:		
Day:		
Day:		
Day:		

Gratitude: being thankful, viewing life as a wonder-filled gift.

Passion & Purpose Miracles Summary

Wk #	Brief summary of miracles and transformations

Miracles: unexpected delights that make you say, "Wow!"

Passion & Purpose Miracles Summary

Wk #	Brief summary of miracles and transformations

Gratitude: being thankful, viewing life as a wonder-filled gift.

Reflection

**What did I learn?
What surprised me?
What would I like to change?**

Miracles: unexpected delights that make you say, "Wow!"

Cycle 12 - Gratitude Supports Optimism & Generosity

"Be grateful for the miracle that is your life. That's the source of generosity, of prosperity, of fulfillment."
--Lynne Twist

Christopher Bergland in *Psychology Today* states, "Recent studies have shown that generosity and gratitude go hand in hand, both at a psychological and neurobiological level. Generosity and gratitude are separate sides of the same coin. They are symbiotic. Fortunately, each of us has the free will to kickstart the neurobiological feedback loop—and upward spiral of well-being—that is triggered by small acts of generosity and gratitude each and every day of our lives. Why not practice a small act of generosity today?"

Find more information about gratitude and optimism and generosity at GratitudeMiracles.com

Gratitude: **being thankful, viewing life as a wonder-filled gift.**

Cycle 12 - Optimism & Generosity

Questions to Ponder:
... How has being optimistic worked in your life?
... Are you generous with your time and money?
... What makes you feel generous?

For a fun and quick test about whether you're an optimist, pessimist or realist, go to http://www.playbuzz.com/jennifers/are-you-an-optimist-a-pessimist-or-a-realist

Write about your own feelings about Optimism & Generosity and feel free to come back to these pages as you go through this cycle.

Miracles: **unexpected delights that make you say, "Wow!"**

Cycle 12 - Gratitude Clarifies Optimism & Generosity

All the prompts, tasks, suggestions, thoughts and tips in the following pages are there simply to stimulate your thinking.

POET is a useful memory trick to help you remember gratitudes related to People, Opportunities, Experiences and Things.

Use them if they're useful; leave them if they're not.

Gratitude: **being thankful, viewing life as a wonder-filled gift.**

Optimism & Generosity Week 1: _____ (Date)

Every day, I will write 3-5 reasons why I'm grateful for ONE thing.
Prompts: sing, spirit, spring, soul, POET* or your choice.

Day of week: _____ I'm grateful for _____

_____

_____

_____

Day of week: _____ It's hard, but I'm grateful for _____

_____

_____

_____

Day of week: _____ I'm grateful for _____

_____

_____

_____

Day of week: _____ I'm grateful for my own _____

_____

_____

_____

Note to self: _____

_____

_____

_____

Cycle 12 - Optimism & Generosity

Miracles: **unexpected delights that make you say, "Wow!"**

*"Optimism is a happiness magnet.
If you stay positive, good things
and good people will be drawn to you."*
-- Mary Lou Retton

Day of week: _____ I'm grateful for _____
_____
_____
_____

Day of week: _____ I'm grateful for _____
_____
_____
_____

Day of week: _____ I'm grateful for _____
_____
_____
_____

Miracles: What miracles and gifts have shown up in my life?
_____
_____

Story: Shortly after my husband died, I was taking a trip with a friend and we were sitting in the Dallas airport. She handed me a silver, plastic fork and began to tell me a story about a family dinner. As the dishes were being cleared, the wise mother told the family to be sure to keep their forks because the "best was yet to come." My friend said, "This fork is to remind you that the best is yet to come for you, too." I still have it, and, she was right. Thank you, Lynne!

Task: Listen to a heart beat and say thanks for the miracle of life.

Gratitude: **being thankful, viewing life as a wonder-filled gift.**

Optimism & Generosity Week 2: _____ (Date)

Every day, I will write 3-5 reasons why I'm grateful for ONE thing.
Prompts: thought, totem, three, triumph, POET* or your choice.

Day of week: _____ I'm grateful for _____

_____

_____

_____

_____

Day of week: _____ It's hard, but I'm grateful for _____

_____

_____

_____

_____

Day of week: _____ I'm grateful for _____

_____

_____

_____

_____

Day of week: _____ I'm grateful for my own _____

_____

_____

_____

Note to self: _____

_____

_____

_____

Miracles: unexpected delights that make you say, "Wow!"

*"Optimism is the faith that leads to achievement.
Nothing can be done without hope and confidence."*
-- Helen Keller

Day of week: _____ I'm grateful for _____

_____

_____

Day of week: _____ I'm grateful for _____

_____

_____

Day of week: _____ I'm grateful for _____

_____

_____

Miracles: What miracles and gifts have shown up in my life?

_____

_____

_____

Thought: Pursuit-of-Happines.com states, "Optimism has been proven to improve the immune system, prevent chronic disease, and help people cope with unfortunate news. Gratitude is associated with optimism and it has been determined that grateful people are happier, receive more social support, are less stressed, and are less depressed."

Task: Thank your parents for something they gave you.

Gratitude: **being thankful, viewing life as a wonder-filled gift.**

Optimism & Generosity Week 3: _____ (Date)

Every day, I will write 3-5 reasons why I'm grateful for ONE thing.
Prompts: useful, ugly, umpire, uniform, POET* or your choice.

Day of week: _____ I'm grateful for _____

Day of week: _____ It's hard, but I'm grateful for _____

Day of week: _____ I'm grateful for _____

Day of week: _____ I'm grateful for my own _____

Note to self: _____

Miracles: **unexpected delights that make you say, "Wow!"**

"Doing a kindness produces the single most reliable momentary increase in well-being of any exercise we have tested."
-- Martin Seligman

Day of week :_____ I'm grateful for _____

Day of week: _____ I'm grateful for _____

Day of week: _____ I'm grateful for _____

Miracles: What miracles and gifts have shown up in my life?

Thought: Martha Beck tells us the Buddha taught that anyone who experiences the delight of being truly generous will never want to eat another meal without sharing it.

Another Thought: From *Fast Company* magazine: "Spending money on others or giving to charity puts a bigger smile on your face than buying things for yourself, according to Michael Norton, a professor at Harvard Business School."

Gratitude: **being thankful, viewing life as a wonder-filled gift.**

Optimism & Generosity Week 4: _____ (Date)

Every day, I will write 3-5 reasons why I'm grateful for ONE thing.
Prompts: vagina, valley, vegetable, verdict, POET* or your choice.

Day of week: _____ I'm grateful for _____

Day of week: _____ It's hard, but I'm grateful for _____

Day of week: _____ I'm grateful for _____

Day of week: _____ I'm grateful for my own _____

Note to self: _____

Miracles: unexpected delights that make you say, "Wow!"

*"Happiness exists on earth
through the constant practice of generosity."*
-- José Marti

Day of week: _____ I'm grateful for _____

_____

_____

_____

Day of week: _____ I'm grateful for _____

_____

_____

_____

Day of week: _____ I'm grateful for _____

_____

_____

_____

Miracles: What miracles and gifts have shown up in my life?

_____

_____

_____

Thought: John O'Donohue, the brilliant Irish poet and philosopher, said, "Once the soul awakens, the search begins and you can never go back. From then on, you are inflamed with a special longing which will never again let you linger in the lowlands of complacency and partial fulfilment.

"When this spiritual path opens, you can bring an incredible generosity to the world and to the lives of others."

Task: Bow to the sun each morning and thank it for its generosity.

Gratitude: being thankful, viewing life as a wonder-filled gift.

Optimism & Generosity Summary:
Brief reminders of gratitudes

	Week 1	Week 2
Day:		
Day:		
Day:		
Day:		
Day:		
Day:		
Day:		

Miracles: unexpected delights that make you say, "Wow!"

Optimism & Generosity Summary:
Brief reminders of gratitudes

	Week 3	Week 4
Day:		
Day:		
Day:		
Day:		
Day:		
Day:		
Day:		

Gratitude: being thankful, viewing life as a wonder-filled gift.

Optimism & Generosity Miracles Summary

Wk #	Brief summary of miracles and transformations

Miracles: unexpected delights that make you say, "Wow!"

Optimism & Generosity Miracles Summary

Wk #	Brief summary of miracles and transformations

Gratitude: **being thankful, viewing life as a wonder-filled gift.**

Reflection

What did I learn?
What surprised me?
What would I like to change?

Miracles: unexpected delights that make you say, "Wow!"

Cycle 13 - Gratitude Encourages Forgiveness

"More Miracles occur from
Gratitude and Forgiveness than anything else."
-- Philip H. Friedman

Forgiveness is not a simple act, nor generally an easy one. Marina Cantacuzino, founder of The Forgiveness Project, says, "All too often we sanitize and simplify forgiveness, when in fact it's an arduous, exhausting task — messy, risky and unpredictable."

For some people, forgiveness is an interpersonal act and requires remorse and a request for forgiveness. For others it's part of a personal, spiritual journey. Author Tony Wilkinson states, "This process (of forgiveness) is part of your inner life, your inner journey and doesn't depend on them (perpetrators), which is why insisting on remorse before forgiveness puts the power in the wrong hands."

This journal addresses the inner journey of forgiveness and does not take the hard work of forgiving lightly.

Find more information about gratitude and forgiveness at GratitudeMiracles.com.

Gratitude: **being thankful, viewing life as a wonder-filled gift.**

Cycle 13 - Forgiveness

Questions to Ponder:
... Are there people or events in your life that you have not been able to forgive?
... Are there actions or events you need to ask forgiveness for?
... Are there things you have not forgiven yourself for? What would it take for you to do that?

Write about your own feelings about Forgiveness and feel free to come back to these pages as you go through this cycle.

Miracles: **unexpected delights that make you say, "Wow!"**

Cycle 13 - Forgiveness

All the prompts, tasks, suggestions, thoughts and tips in the following pages are there simply to stimulate your thinking.

POET is a useful memory trick to help you remember gratitudes related to People, Opportunities, Experiences and Things.

Use them if they're useful; leave them if they're not.

For a beautiful short video on forgiveness, see
http://gratituderevealed.com/portfolio/forgiveness/

Gratitude: **being thankful, viewing life as a wonder-filled gift.**

Forgiveness Week 1: _____ (Date)

Every day, I will write 3-5 reasons why I'm grateful for ONE thing.
Prompts: wheel, wind, write, women, POET* or your choice.

Day of week: _____ I'm grateful for _____
_____
_____
_____
_____

Day of week: _____ It's hard, but I'm grateful for _____
_____
_____
_____
_____

Day of week: _____ I'm grateful for _____
_____
_____
_____
_____

Day of week: _____ I'm grateful for my own _____
_____
_____
_____

Note to self: _____
_____
_____
_____

Miracles: **unexpected delights that make you say, "Wow!"**

"Forgiveness is a form of gratitude. When we forgive others, we show them the mercy that we have often received and been thankful for."
-- Sarah Ban Breathnach

Day of week: _____ I'm grateful for _____

_____

_____

_____

Day of week: _____ I'm grateful for _____

_____

_____

_____

Day of week: _____ I'm grateful for _____

_____

_____

_____

Miracles: What miracles and gifts have shown up in my life?

_____

_____

_____

Story: Archbishop Desmond Tutu, who said, "Without forgiveness there is no future," chaired the South African Truth and Reconciliation Commission in a remarkable process of forgiveness and healing. Victims of gross human rights violations were invited to give statements about their experiences, and perpetrators of violence could express remorse and request amnesty from both civil and criminal prosecution.

Task: Breathe in peace and reconciliation. Breathe out gratitude.

Gratitude: **being thankful, viewing life as a wonder-filled gift.**

Forgiveness Week 2: _____ (Date)

Every day, I will write 3-5 reasons why I'm grateful for ONE thing.
Prompts: celebrate, drum, smile, fortune, POET* or your choice.

Day of week:_____ I'm grateful for _____
_____
_____
_____

Day of week: _____ It's hard, but I'm grateful for _____
_____
_____
_____

Day of week:_____ I'm grateful for _____
_____
_____
_____

Day of week: _____ I'm grateful for my own _____
_____
_____
_____

Note to self: _____
_____
_____
_____

Miracles: **unexpected delights that make you say, "Wow!"**

"The way of forgiveness is the way of gratitude and astonishment. It lets the past become our teacher rather than our judge."
-- John Claypool

Day of week: _____ I'm grateful for _____

_____

_____

Day of week: _____ I'm grateful for _____

_____

_____

Day of week: _____ I'm grateful for _____

_____

_____

Miracles: What miracles and gifts have shown up in my life?

_____

_____

Thought: Relationship coach Larry James says, "Forgiveness is an act of the imagination. It dares you to imagine a better future, one that is based on the blessed possibility that your hurt will not be the final word on the matter. It challenges you to give up your destructive thoughts about the situation and to believe in the possibility of a better future. It builds confidence that you can survive the pain and grow from it."

Task: Forgive yourself for something you did, or failed to do, in the past.

Gratitude: **being thankful, viewing life as a wonder-filled gift.**

Forgiveness Week 3: _____ (Date)

Every day, I will write 3-5 reasons why I'm grateful for ONE thing.
Prompts: yearn, yard, year, yesterday, POET* or your choice.

Day of week: _____ I'm grateful for _____

_____
_____
_____
_____

Day of week: _____ It's hard, but I'm grateful for _____

_____
_____
_____
_____

Day of week: _____ I'm grateful for _____

_____
_____
_____
_____

Day of week: _____ I'm grateful for my own _____

_____
_____
_____

Note to self: _____

_____
_____
_____

***Miracles:* unexpected delights that make you say, "Wow!"**

*"Not forgiving is like drinking rat poison
and then waiting for the rat to die."*
-- Anne Lamott

Day of week :_____ I'm grateful for _____

_____
_____
_____

Day of week: _____ I'm grateful for _____

_____
_____
_____

Day of week: _____ I'm grateful for _____

_____
_____
_____

Miracles: What miracles and gifts have shown up in my life?

_____
_____
_____

Thought: Fred Luskin, Director of the Stanford University Forgiveness Projects, states, "Forgiveness requires gratitude. I teach forgiveness, but at the heart of forgiveness, I see that most of us have issues with gratitude and compassion. If you had a real thankfulness for your very life; if you could touch the sacred mystery of being here, it would be staggering.

"The other problem is that if you don't forgive, then you are in some ways prejudging your future - that you are on guard and defended and helpless, that there's a residual bitterness that influences your capacity for happiness because you haven't resolved something from your past."

Gratitude: **being thankful, viewing life as a wonder-filled gift.**

Forgiveness Week 4: _____ (Date)

Every day, I will write 3-5 reasons why I'm grateful for ONE thing.
Prompts: zero, zebra, zoo, zinc, POET* or your choice.

Day of week: _____ I'm grateful for _____
_____
_____
_____
_____

Day of week: _____ It's hard, but I'm grateful for _____
_____
_____
_____
_____

Day of week: _____ I'm grateful for _____
_____
_____
_____
_____

Day of week: _____ I'm grateful for my own _____
_____
_____
_____

Note to self: _____
_____
_____
_____

Miracles: **unexpected delights that make you say, "Wow!"**

*"The practice of forgiveness is our most important
contribution to the healing of the world."*
-- Marianne Williamson

Day of week: _____ I'm grateful for _____

_____

_____

Day of week: _____ I'm grateful for _____

_____

_____

Day of week: _____ I'm grateful for _____

_____

_____

Miracles: What miracles and gifts have shown up in my life?

_____

_____

Thought: *Positive Psychology News* reports, "Forgiveness is the flip side of gratitude." Psychologist Robert Enright defines forgiveness as, "The foregoing of resentment or revenge when the wrongdoer's actions deserve it and instead giving the offender gifts of mercy, generosity and love or beneficence when the wrongdoer does not deserve them.

"In other words, when people forgive, they essentially give up the anger to which they are entitled and give to their offender a gift to which he or she is not entitled."

So, forgiveness requires generosity which is stimulated by gratitude!

Gratitude: being thankful, viewing life as a wonder-filled gift.

Forgiveness Summary:
Brief reminders of gratitudes

	Week 1	Week 2
Day:		
Day:		
Day:		
Day:		
Day:		
Day:		
Day:		

Miracles: unexpected delights that make you say, "Wow!"

Forgiveness Summary:
Brief reminders of gratitudes

	Week 3	Week 4
Day:		
Day:		
Day:		
Day:		
Day:		
Day:		
Day:		

Gratitude: being thankful, viewing life as a wonder-filled gift.

Forgiveness Miracles Summary

Wk #	Brief summary of miracles and transformations

Miracles: unexpected delights that make you say, "Wow!"

Forgiveness Miracles Summary

Wk #	Brief summary of miracles and transformations

Gratitude: being thankful, viewing life as a wonder-filled gift.

Reflection

**What did I learn?
What surprised me?
What would I like to change?**

Miracles: unexpected delights that make you say, "Wow!"

If you have come this far,

you deserve

a huge

I would love to hear

from you ...

Comment on

GratitudeMiracles.com

or

email me at

jwycoff@me.com

Gratitude: **being thankful, viewing life as a wonder-filled gift.**

Made in the USA
Las Vegas, NV
16 March 2023